Snake Oil

Snake Oil

Life's Calculations,
Misdirections, and Manipulations

Jim Rose

Bartleby Press
Silver Spring, Maryland

Cover portrait of Jim Rose by Gail Potocki

Printed in the United States of America

Bartleby Press
9045 Maier Road
Laurel, MD 20723
800-953-9929
www.BartlebythePublisher.com

Learn more about Jim Rose at www.JimRoseCircus.com

Library of Congress Cataloging-in-Publication Data

Rose, Jim, 1956-
    Snake oil : life's calculations, misdirections, and manipulations / Jim Rose.
       p. cm.
    ISBN: 0-910155-59-3
    ISBN-13: 978-0-910155-59-5
    1. Swindlers and swindling. 2. Carnival games. 3. Impostors and imposture. 4. Tricks. 5. Manipulative behavior. 6. Deception. I. Title.

HV6691.R67 2004
364.16'3—dc22

                                    2004018678

CONTENTS

ACKNOWLEDGEMENTS

A special thanks to the Jim Rose Research and Development team:

Bébé Rose: Vice-President and Coordinating Director
Dean Wynveen: Assistant Vice-President
Stephan Soule: Research And Advice
Isaac Louie: Research And Advice
James Taylor: Source Direction
Johnny Meah: Source Direction
Ward Hall: Source Direction
Sheila Lyon: Source Direction
Larry Reid: Project Overview
Jeff Crawford: Environment Specialist
Mark Constantino: Golf Instructor
Fred Riley aka Romance Jones: Legal
John "The God Father" Branigan: Super Agent, William Morris Agency
Rob Markus: Euro Ops
Gail Potocki: Artist who did cover painting
Tom Negovan: Confidant

DISCLAIMER

The contents of this book are dangerous. Misuse of the material can cheapen an art form or at the very least make you look stupid. More importantly, misuse of this information may result in jail time or death. Do not attempt any of these tricks without the direct supervision of a responsible professional.

INTRODUCTION

I know more about snake oil than any person alive. I've been selling it for most of my life. Quite simply, snake oil is my lifeblood. Magic, circus stunts, hypnotism, hustles, mind-reading; any and every graft known to man. If there's a con, I know about it. Snake oil, ladies and gentlemen, is the art of the gyp, hoodwink, shuck, sandbag. Identify a weakness or susceptibility and manipulate to your personal advantage. The term originates from traveling "salesmen" in the 19th century who peddled a concoction, usually giving it an exotic name like snake oil, promising to cure all ills. Of course, it was a big scam and eventually the term snake oil came to represent any deceptive product or enterprise.

Growing up in Phoenix, Arizona, life's calculations, misdirections, and manipulations became a fascination of mine. During this semi-lawless era reminiscent of the Wild West, slicksters, con-artists, and hucksters roamed the terrain looking for easy marks. Phoenix has now, I've been told, become quite civilized and the days of flim-flam are long gone. Don't believe it. The art of selling snake oil is constantly being reinvented, bastardized and ultimately improved in a perpetual, strangely perverse evolution. Just like me.

My introduction to the swindle of snake oil began during my formative teenage years. Working at the state fair, I was initiated into the world of eccentrics with a school-of-hard-knocks education in street smarts. In the late eighties, this education allowed me to found the *Jim Rose Circus*, touring the planet non-stop for fifteen years. During this odyssey of the odd, I became part of a living eclectic encyclopedia. I have also been to two world fairs and have seen Rocky Mountain goats copulate, so I'm definitely qualified to write this book. In fact, no one alive is *more* qualified.

Much of the information you will find in this offering is oral history passed along from hustler to hustler; con artist to con artist; huckster to huckster. By capturing this knowledge in these pages, I've ensured that it won't be lost forever. It might seem like a dubious legacy, yes, but I'm confident it will stand the test of time.

The roots of all business and magic can be found in the rook of snake oil. But this is not a "How To" book intended to encourage anarchists, con men or entertainers. Its purpose is to help the brain think in terms of angles.

This collection of the strange and risky is not exclusive to Americana. Many of the puzzle pieces have been culled from the weirdness of Belgium, Scandinavia, Germany, the U.K., France, Austria, Holland, Switzerland, Spain, Jamaica, New Zealand, Australia and South Africa.

There's an interesting theory I'll propose for your consideration. Until the age of about fifty, your head stores itself full with info. After fifty, nature reverses to do some intellectual house cleaning. This process continues until all of the brain's creases are ironed and polished to the point of not even being able to control drool.

One of the reasons I wrote this book now was to preserve some of the interesting clutter before remembering it all became too overwhelming. Another reason stemmed from my frustrations associated with research. And my fear of drooling.

My research on mind control serves as a representative example. Brainwashing can be explained clearly in two paragraphs. Or you can take the time to devour a 300 page tome on the subject. Complete it and you're more confused than when you started. Authors are often guilty of turning a paragraph into hundreds of pages and calling it a book. Some of the subjects in this book fall under this category. Distilling topics with clarity and brevity provides an insightful overview of the craft of snake oil. It starts with this introduction you're reading now.

Snake oil. I've learned from the best. Been burned by the worst. Along the way, I've even contributed a few of my own inventions. Come and get it . . . There's nothing it won't cure.

ENTERTAINING ANIMALS

So You Want to Bullfight?

Here are some rules for this deathly feat of animal cruelty. If you ever thought of becoming a matador, I hope these realities dissuade you. In Spain, anybody can visit private ranches that raise fighting bulls and learn how to face them. In these amateur arenas heifers are used in place of bulls, and there are no killings, but this prepares you for the next level and teaches you graceful bravery skills.

These hints won't make you a professional matador, but if you've ever been interested in the subject, this should help.

#1: While learning and practicing, the points of the horns should be filed or sawed off.

#2: Use the small cape (called "muleta"). It is a piece of flannel attached to a two-foot wooden stick that serves as a handle.

#3: All bulls do not like running into walls because in their life experience they have found that it hurts.

Walk parallel to the heifer with the cape wide open, and keep your back to the wall. When you're fifteen feet away from the animal, shake the cape and shout "Hey bull." His reaction will be to charge. Face the animal and have the cape extended in his path. Do not move! The color and size of the cape will attract the heifer. While he's charging, don't do anything that will distract him from the cloth. Once the animal goes through it, don't just stand there, but be prepared for the second charge. Move three or four steps back to give you more room in case of a sudden charge.

If he's slow and is just looking around, you can provoke a charge by moving a step towards the center of the ring shaking the cape.

You gain points with style and fearlessness.

Repeat this act a few more times, then retire to the safety of the protective barriers.

Now you see how hard it is to kill a cow. I hope you've lost interest. Olé!

While we're on the subject of animal cruelty, here are some more examples:

Kangaroo Boxing and Other Animal Stunts

The red male roo is the largest of the kangaroo family; he stands over six feet tall. The fists are not your problem because he will balance on the back of his tail and use his powerful bottom feet to spring you into next week.

Ever wanted to *fight a monkey*? Back in the fifties, before lawsuits flourished and it was deemed cruelty to man, they had ape fighting. Anyone who got rough with a gorilla, had their clothes ripped off and became humiliated in the nude.

It's what happens when you get whipped around like a rag doll.

Ever wanted to *dance with a stripper monkey*? Animals don't want to wear clothing, but monkeys can do something about it. They can take them off. So, after you've dressed your monkey, quickly put the music on and cha-cha-cha.

It's easier to *dance with a chicken*. Put a little piece of Scotch tape under one of its feet, and watch it kick.

Now let's get back to old-time animal challenges: The scariest of them all has to be *bear wrestling*. I have never seen or heard of a legitimate contest ever taking place. When a bear wrestling act hits town, drunken frat boys goad each other into the ring. Once there, they look across and see a big, real, live bear. So they usually dance around a little bit and run out of the ring.

Some circuses make their *elephants* turn left or right by using a marksman hidden in the rafters to shoot them with a BB gun on cue. Ouch, you jerk!

Python Death Grip

This one is extremely dangerous but skilled professionals can take a big breath, flex their arms at their sides to become as large as possible. They hold this position while the snake wraps around them. When they feel the first squeeze, they exhale and move their arms to the front of their body, causing the snake to re-constrict. This is the moment they can fight their way out.

Animals Can be Hypnotized

Guinea Pig:

Make it dizzy by rolling it around for a couple of seconds, then place it on its back. It should remain still until you blow on its nose.

Lobster:

Make it rest on its claws by holding the tail up until it becomes completely still. To get it to stop snoring, just put it back on its feet and let go.

Frog:

Put it on its back and hold it in that position for a few seconds. Carefully remove your hand, and you'll see the frog sleeping. To stop the effect, snap your fingers and quickly flip it back onto its feet.

Rabbit:

Place it on its back and pin it down by putting one hand on the ears and the other on the back legs.

Expect the rabbit not to like this, but do not let go until you feel the final quiver. This usually takes about 30 seconds. But hey, if you're doing this you must have all day to waste! To bring the rabbit out of its nightmare, roll it on its side and give a good puff on the nose; it will hop away to tell all its friends.

Chicken:

Grab the chicken by the neck, force its head down onto a table, take a piece of chalk and draw a two-foot straight line starting from the beak. Let go and it will not move. To get your chicken to stop counting sheep, erase the line and clap your hands close to its head.

Reminder: If you have been dancing with the chicken ahead of time, do not forget to remove the tape!

Alligator Jumping

In Florida, at the Gator Jamboree, they get alligators to jump by holding a chicken on a hook over their heads. The alligators don't seem to care whether or not the chicken is hypnotized or has tape on its foot.

Flea Cruelty?

When it comes to a flea circus, presentation is ninety-nine percent of the act. The circus pitch Bobby Reynolds used goes roughly like this: "Ladies and gentlemen, I am a flea tamer and it's not easy gaining the confidence of a flea like that of a cricket or spider. A flea is a parasite that has been hunted since the beginning of mankind. It's very hard to get them to trust you. See Marcus and Caesar in a chariot being pulled by their slaves. All of the circus equipment is run by fleas. See the gorgeous Betty, world's greatest dancing flea; she will lift up her dress and let you see her legs. Even the small are great to those who know them."

Well I know them. A flea circus is just a bunch of miniature canons, tanks and chariots being pulled around by fleas tied to a thread. The way to train them is to put them in a thin canister until they're tired of banging their heads and stop jumping. The hard part is to tie a knot around their waist with the thread. Some flea circuses don't even have fleas. They're so small, no one can tell.

Bear Bicycling

Getting a bear to ride a bicycle is easy. Getting a bear, well, that's another story!

Put a stationary bicycle in your encampment. Bears are naturally curious, and will play with it. In a couple of weeks, they will advance to pedaling. At that point bring in a real bicycle with large training wheels. After they get used to that, take the training wheels off and stay out of their way for a while.

Mouse in Wheel

This is a popular betting game on the midway of carnivals and state fairs. A large wheel is divided into sections numbered from 1 to 60, with a small hole in each numbered section. The operator puts a mouse in a cup and puts it inside the wheel which is spun energetically. The operator then removes the cup from the dizzy mouse that runs to one of the numbered holes for safety. Anybody who bets that number wins. But it seems that the mouse always plays against the bettors.

Secret: Like lots of other carnival games, this one became crooked. There is a mechanical gadget under the wheel that closes every other hole. The operator checks the betting at the counter. If heavy betting is on the odd numbers, he closes them, and if there are more bets on the even numbers, he does the opposite. Once released, the dizzy mouse will seek out the first hole it can find.

Cruelty to Man

There was this guy who had been seeking employment for over a year. One day he walked into a zoo to apply for a job. The zoo keeper said: "I don't have regular jobs, but I sure need a gorilla. I'll give you ten dollars an hour if you'll put on this gorilla outfit and act like a monkey in cage # 3." After a couple of days, the guy got sick of being a gorilla. It wasn't like he thought it would be. They never let him out of the cage and would only feed him and give him water through the bars. So he decided to escape. He climbed to the top of the cage, flipped his legs over the top and started to climb down. But he slipped and fell into the lion's den. He freaked out and started running to the door in the feline's compound, screaming: "Help, help, help!" The lions heard this, and started to chase him. He got to the gate and screamed louder than ever, "Please help! Help! I'm going to be eaten."

The lions were getting closer and closer. Finally they were right on top of him and he screamed one last time before hearing the lions say: "SSHH, be quiet or you'll get us all fired!"

Squirrelly Cat

If squirrels are nesting in your attic, place a radio up there. The high volume will drive them away. If they are in your fireplace, put a bucket of ammonia at the bottom; the fumes will rise which will also make them leave.

Some people hate it when cats walk in their yards so they push toothpicks halfway into the ground all along their fence. When the cats step on the tooth-pick it stings their paws. After experiencing this form of animal cruelty a few times they will find another yard.

Devices & Sleights
for Deception

Mentalists are very entertaining with the mystery surrounding them and their amazing predictions. Be careful of the ones who act like they possess supernatural powers. Most of their tricks are done with magic apparatus.

Most of the tricks described in this book are done with magic apparatus. A few of them can only be accomplished with a basic understanding of these gimmicks.

Blindfolds

The most common blindfold is just a regular four inch wide by ten inch long piece of satin or velvet with an elastic band sewn on each side that keeps the blindfold comfortably tight around the head. You can't see through straight, but if you frown and raise the eyebrows while it's placed on top of your eyes, you can see very well down your nose.

Another blindfold that can be used is a regular *handkerchief* or bandana. Fold it by rolling two opposite corners toward each other, leaving a one inch gap in the middle so you can see through one thickness of fabric. See illustration:

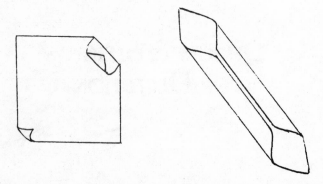

Magic stores sell *tricked blindfolds*. For example one mask has two tiny holes that can't be seen by the audience. When holding this mask, make sure that no bright light is behind you, or it will show through the holes.

Some mediums use a *blanket* or sheet for a blindfold, but in fact they don't want to be seen. This pretty much allows them to do something like using a small flashlight to read or write messages.

In other cases, mentalists use a *bag* put over their head. The way it works is by sewing two bags together, a thick one inside a thin one with one side unsewn. When putting the bag on, they peel the thick unsewn layer back leaving them with just the thin bag that is easy to see through.

The same principle can be achieved by using two bags; the thick one is examined by the audience, and at the opportune time, they switch with the second one which is thin enough to see through. You need good sleight of hand for this one.

The bag blindfold is usually used by performers who need glasses to see but prefer not to wear them on stage. The glasses are placed inside the bag beforehand; the performer puts them on when his head is inside the bag, and leaves them there when removing it. Personally, I like using the blindfolds given by the airlines. They work perfectly.

A novel approach to the blindfold act is to put a *bucket* over your head. Make sure you can see well through it before using it in public, or those around you will sense your blindness and have a good old time slapping the bucket around! Normally that would be okay; there is very little chance of getting hurt, but since your ears are in there, the incredible noise could make you go deaf. In any case this unorthodox approach could be very good for breaking the ice, and you have a bucket to put it in!

As for everything else, practice a few times with any blindfold so that the routine looks good. Don't be obvious, since you can see through it, don't forget to act like you can't!

Remember one thing, with any blindfold, have your eyes closed before putting it on and when taking it off. This little trick psychologically seals the deal for the audience.

Swami Gimmicks

These apparatus are widely used for predictions when you pretend to write something beforehand. The writing is actually done with these devices while the choice is made. There are different varieties to suit everyone's finger and/or need depending on the trick.

The Thumb Tip: Made of plastic, rubber or aluminum, it is shaped to fit over the thumb and is painted flesh colored. It is used to conceal or switch scarves, lit cigarettes, rolled dollar bills, etc.

The Thumb Tip Writer: It is a thumb tip that has a small pencil lead attached to the end of the thumb for writing. There are different types depending on the position of the lead. It can be placed on the tip or underneath the thumb. It has to fit well enough so that it is easy to put on and take off. Choose the one that will give you the most comfort and control when writing. Make sure the lead is not too long or it will break. I suggest to secure it by gluing it; this will prevent it from pushing inside the tip when you write.

You can find other varieties of "nail writers" at your local magic shop. Some in the shape of a half ring will fit under the nail, others slip under the index or thumb with the help of adhesive, etc.

When handling one of these devices, act naturally, since you're the only one aware of it, don't draw attention to it. If you're not wearing it already for the trick, make sure that you have easy access during the performance. To be safe, always carry two of them on you in case one is lost or the lead breaks.

Sleight of Hand

Palming: It is probably the most basic and necessary skill a conjurer can possess. Coins, cigarettes, and cards can magically disappear, and dice can be switched if you know how to do the simple sleight of hand.

When sitting around with nothing to do, practice holding objects cupped in the palm of your hand. Then comes the harder part of holding the object naturally without people seeing it.

Human Blockhead

A human blockhead is someone who pounds a spike or a nail into his face. He takes advantage of the public's general lack of anatomical knowledge. In each nostril there are two nasal cavities: one that goes up, and the other used in the act that goes straight back into the head.

A blockhead often starts with a small nail and roots around in his nose, familiarizing himself with the terrain. Once he gets over the watery eyes and desire to sneeze, he works his way up to larger nails.

Dice Switch

Switching dice is relatively simple. Curl your little finger and the one next to it around the loaded dice. Pick up the thrown dice with the remaining two fingers and thumb. Pretend to shake up and let the loaded dice go.

Borrowed Hair

The fakir shows a long human hair and has a knot tied in it. Several people can try to untie the same knot but they will fail. Fakir does so with ease.

Secret: Knot is tied, not too tightly so as to split the hair, but closely. Hair is placed in the hand across the base of the little finger and nipped there. Palm of the opposite hand is placed over and the back of the hand lightly nipping the hair is struck sharply against the knees a number of times. On examining the hair, the knot will be found sufficiently loose to pass ends through and untie.

Yogi Ribbon Stunt

During this act, someone, typically a yogi, eats a ribbon, goes through stomach gyrations, then pulls out the ribbon from the hole in his abdomen, making it appear as though it's gone the fast track through the digestive system.

Secret: This stunt is based on an illusion. Typically the performer already has a piercing situated an inch to the left of the belly button. And in that hole he has placed a second identical ribbon, which he pulls out after swallowing the first.

Straitjacket Escape

Unfortunately, there are fake devices that can give their user's audience the illusion of witnessing a human marvel. There are gimmick ones available that anybody can get out of. Real straitjackets, however, are still available and can be ordered through the Humane Restraint Company of Waunakee, Wisconsin. Contrary to popular belief an escape artist doesn't pop a shoulder to get out. This stunt relies on a pretzel movement of the arm: an escape artist puts the top arm over the head, the other arm behind his back, and curlicues out of it. An insane person wouldn't figure this out; but straitjacket escape is relatively easy for those who can understand the pretzel logic.

Regurgitation

One of Houdini's tricks to escape from jail was to swallow a key to the top of the gag reflex, and to bring it back up at will.

This skill relies on modifying the swallowing process. Everyone has had a chunk of food stuck in the throat and had to go through the unpleasant experience of working it back up. Regurgitators tease and provoke this mechanism intentionally, practicing with rolled up balls of bread.

Alligator-Skin Man

This is another act you could see inside shows where a man looked like an alligator. The effect was done by dumping glue all over the body and letting it dry and crack until it appears scaly enough to be the alligator man.

Astral Control

The Hindu has been seen to cause a rubber ball or balloon to follow him around the room merely by placing the fingertips on it. This secret is very simple, but also little known. Stroke an inflated balloon with a silk handkerchief. This places charge on the surface. As the charge on the balloon is attracted to neutral bodies, it will readily approach the hand extended toward it. Under the best conditions, it may even follow a person around the room until the charge is dissipated.

Ghandi's East Indian Miracle

Termed a miracle effect, this should be appreciated by performers seeking unusual effects. Every magician and mystery entertainer wants to be different, wants to be able to give himself a distinctive reputation. Being different isn't necessarily being original. This effect does fall in the seemingly impossible class. In your Editor's opinion, it was undoubtedly used by disloyal draftees during the war and undoubtedly proved a puzzle to many doctors. It can be done almost impromptu and used as a full act, a spirit test, or a test of mediumship. It is possible to obtain wide publicity with it, but it should be remembered that this feat, like all the feats described in these pages is not a plaything, and the method should be taken seriously and so respected.

The body temperature is made to rise several degrees and the heart to beat at a rapid rate. The astute performer would present this to a news office for publicity before a group of doctors. The effect should be followed exactly as described.

Take a piece of common yellow laundry soap about the size of a quarter and eat it. Follow this by drinking a cup of hot tea. That is all there is to it. The rest works itself. After a few minutes the body temperature will start upward and the pulse beat will increase. This condition will stay with you for a period of about twenty-five hours or less. No amount of examination can disclose the means used.

It can be readily seen that the very simplicity makes this a crushing masterpiece for publicity work. The soap may taste terrible, but the spectators will think you're wonderful. Nearly all Hindu effects are based on seemingly absurd methods. But it is absurd methods that create sensations.

This effect came from a real Hindu mystic. After the demonstration the performer should rest until the effects of his dosing subsides.

Where's The Beat?

Here's a great feat where the pulse is supposedly stopped by using willpower.

Here is the secret: Beforehand, secure a tennis ball under your naked armpit. Ask someone from the audience to locate and feel your pulse beat. Tell him to signal as soon as he doesn't feel it anymore. Now secretly press your arm on the ball. This will apply a steady pressure against the artery supplying the pulse. The person will therefore feel the pulse slowly stopping.

When the pressure of the arm reaches a certain level, the pulse beat will no longer be felt, and the spectator will signal to the audience that the beat has ceased. Then slowly release the pressure on the ball to make the pulse beat come back.

This effect is usually used in trance scams.

The Babylonian Mystery

Also known as the "Power of the Orient," this is a little known and interesting scientific fact and makes a novel demonstration. Performer patters about the control of the mind through hypnotism. Both human beings and animals are subject to these mystic powers. And now, he says, he can control flowers! To prove this statement, he passes his hands over a bouquet of flowers and they visibly wilt!

The secret of this unusual effect lies in the application of an anesthetic to the flowers. The scientific laboratories have noted that flowers, too, are subject to sleep producing drugs as well as human beings. Carnations are considered the best subject and the spray used for it is a spray that the performer has concealed in his coat sleeve is ethylene chloride. It is said that only one part in 18,000,000 will influence the carnations. Other anesthetics have been used, such as ether and chloroform.

Presented in a proper setting and manner, with an air of mystery worked into the patter, this can be quite effective.

HYPNOTISM, MIND CONTROL, AND OTHER MYSTERIOUS FEATS

Hypnotism, brain washing, and mind control are the same thing. The only difference is how the knowledge is used.

I read lots of books on hypnotism when I was a kid but couldn't grasp what they meant. I ended up learning through trial, error, and by watching others. Recently after thousands of hours of experimenting in shows, I started to study again, and everything became clearer. I learned that most people don't walk outside one day saying they're going to join a cult. They run into someone who knows how to use the two keys of mind control: unfamiliar environment and forceful suggestions. Con men, pimps and high pressure salesmen are under the same umbrella; these basic human manipulations are considered a folk art.

Stage Hypnotism

The "unfamiliar environment" starts the minute the volunteer gets on stage. Lights are in his eyes, the audience is staring at him, some are friends but most are not. A stage hypnotist has a microphone that makes his forceful suggestion more powerful. It's easier to go along with what he says than to buck the system. The long "look into my eyes" presentation is used to disguise the hypnotist's abrasiveness and unspoken agreement that he is the director and the volunteer is the actor.

Private Hypnotists use a bright light and matched and amplified breathing sound loops in their sessions to help people to stop smoking, drinking, etc.

Easy Way Out

I have done a legitimate hypnotist act for many years and have made people do a lot of crazy things.

One night this cocky guy volunteered, but wouldn't focus no matter what I tried. I couldn't get him to look me in the eyes, so off the microphone I told him to just play along and I would give him a hundred dollars after the show. He immediately started doing everything I told him. He acted like a dog, a chicken, he caressed his breasts as though they were a woman's, and rolled around on the floor like a pig in the mud. After I was through letting him humiliate himself, I said to him: "And now before I count to three and bring you out of hypnosis, I want to leave you with one powerful thought. For the rest of your life, you will believe and tell your friends that Jim Rose owes you money. 1, 2, 3. Give him a big hand." He went back to his chair telling his friends that I owed him one hundred dollars. He probably still is!

Easier Way Out

If you don't want to bother learning hypnotism, I've seen people make this trick work. They show the audience a 12x12 inch piece of cardboard with a hypnotic spiral drawn on it. What the audience doesn't see is the other side shown to the volunteers. It says, "Just play along and let's have fun" written on the back. The audience assumes the hypnotic spiral is on both sides.

Controlling Power

This, too, is a weird effect capable of dramatic presentation. In brief, the performer convinces his subjects that they are tasting candy. Later, that they have tasted bitter medicine.

Secret: Apparatus used is nothing more than a little novelty known as a platelifter or palpitator. This is a length of thin rubber tubing with a small bulb at one end and a small bladder at the other. To use, the bladder is removed and a small quantity of saccharine placed in the bulb. Saccharine is obtainable from any drug store, the powder form being used, and is several hundred times sweeter than sugar. The bulb is placed under the armpit and the tube is fastened to the arm with rubber bands.

In "hypnotizing" his subjects the performer makes his "mesmeric passes" and in so doing presses lightly on the rubber bulb so that a little of the powder is sprayed forth. Just a little of this, in fact the very smallest amount coming in contact with the subject's lips will cause an intensely sweet taste to be produced in the mouth of the spectator. Meanwhile the performer suggests that the taste is that of candy.

In the medicine tasting part of the test the same saccharine is used. Immediately after the candy test, this thought is produced, since saccharine will leave a bitter taste if the sweet persists long enough. During this time the performer continues his patter and builds up to this final effect.

If desired, the opposite arm can be likewise prepared with a setup containing sneezing powder or itching powder. Thus by suggestion alone the spectator will be led to sneeze, or being shown a picture of poison ivy, be led to itch. These tricks have long been closely guarded.

Pulse Control

Place a hard rubber ball under the right armpit in direct contact with the flesh. Hold the arm extended from the elbow and have a spectator feel your pulse. Tell him your pulse will gradually fade away. Gradually press on the ball with the arm and the flow of blood will be stopped, and naturally the pulse will diminish and seem to practically fade away. This is very effective for trance work in seances.

High Pressure

Let's take the example of the truck driving schools. They advertise that you can make over four thousand dollars a month after one week of training. The minute you walk in, the process of fleecing starts. You stand behind a red line until you are waved up to a guy who is sitting on a platform behind a six-foot high black counter. The first thing he'll say is: "Let me see your driver's license." A light is positioned to shine in your eyes as you look up to follow his forceful suggestion to hand over your license. He then asks: "What makes you think you can be a truck driver?" After answering the question you have started a pattern of following instructions that will last until the unfamiliar environment and forceful suggestions work their way into your wallet.

Your Future

The so-called psychic can't read your mind or tell your future with accuracy. It's all a formula. First they shake your hand to feel if it is rough or smooth. They study your clothes, jewelry, appearance of health, and whether you're calm or nervous. They are very good listeners, so they can use the information later, but they never ask direct questions. The goal is to find your main interest. It's usually money, health, or sex. Then they build a story around a positive point. They try to make you say "yes" as much as possible. For example, if someone asks a question like: "Is my daughter going to get engaged?" The conversation might go: "I believe you're a married woman." "Yes." "Therefore you will appreciate what I will say. First, let me ask you, or better tell you, that I feel your problem does concern a marriage, although it has not yet taken place." "Yes." "I'd say that there is in fact an engagement with a view to marriage in the air." "Yes." "Now, let me deal with a gentleman who has a very great bearing on this matter. There is a great deal of personal feeling for him in the family." "Yes."

Psychics feed back facts, and act like they have made a discovery. The worldly ones can help you relax and give good advice. That's why I still have my future read.

Bad Fortune

Be careful of fortune tellers who say that your money problems can be solved with a spell. After several sessions, and gaining your confidence, they will ask you to bring in 500 dollars cash for a cleansing ritual. They take your money and sew it in a handkerchief while reciting incantations and using magic powders. They wrap a strand of hair around it and tell you to sleep with it under your pillow for a week. Of course a week later upon opening the handkerchief, you'll find just paper.

The fortune teller had a duplicate made ahead of time, and switched it with sleight of hand.

Cold as Hot

This effect is based on the power of suggestion. Ask a volunteer to stand erect and keep his hands behind his back. A blindfold is placed over his eyes. Tell him that you will place a hot pin in the palm of his hand, and instruct him to tell you to stop when the pain is unbearable.

After he's blindfolded, light a match as if you're going to burn a pin. He will hear it and smell the match, but instead of touching his hand with the hot pin, touch it with an ice cube. You will notice that he'll tell you right away it's too hot.

Trick Yourself

Is there something in your personality that you would like to change? Self-hypnosis can trick your brain to accomplish this. Before going out and buying a book about it or getting involved with courses, try this for three weeks. Let's say you want more self-confidence. Every morning, afternoon, and just before you go to bed, repeat "bold and confident" over and over to yourself for five straight minutes. Concentrating on nothing else but "bold and confident" three times a day is a mental strain that you're not used to. Self-suggestions swim right through and become a part of your personality within a couple of weeks.

I know there are all kinds of jokes about self-help books, but I won't tell if you won't.

On Stage

Georgia Magnet

Hold a broomstick in front of you with both hands, and ask a volunteer to push against it to throw you off balance. Because of your "mystic powers" the person will lose his strength and won't be able to budge you.

Secret: First of all, to make this experiment more impressive, choose a strong man. Hold a broomstick horizontally about one foot away from your chest, the hands placed wider than your shoulders, arms bent at a 90 degree angle. Ask the volunteer to stand in front of you, and to grab the stick at each end. Now tell him to press against the broomstick to push you over without any jerking.

If you keep the broom close to your chest and always push up, he won't be able to knock you over.

Devilish Broomstick

Hold a broom above the bristles vertically in front of you and two feet above the floor.

Ask five volunteers to hold the top of the broom. Now challenge them to push the broom downward until the bristles touch the floor.

No matter how hard they try, they won't be able to do it, even though there are five people against one.

Secret: To swerve the downward energy, move the broom slightly to either the left or the right. It will make them push sideways and not downward.

Vanishing Glass

This trick makes a glass disappear through a table while the audience is paying attention to a quarter.

It is important this is done while you're sitting at the end of a table, or sitting where no one has a view from the side.

Place a quarter pretty close to the edge of a table and put the glass upside down covering it. Now say: "We can see the coin through the glass and hear it rattle when I move the glass back and forth. If I wrap a paper bag on top of the glass, we can't see the quarter, but we can still hear it if I move the glass. When I lift the wrapped glass up, we can still see the coin."

While doing this, bring attention to the quarter. Repeat this move a few times to set them up. The second time secretly let the glass fall gently onto your lap. The wrapping will maintain the frame of the glass and appears as though it is still inside. Set the empty wrapper back onto the quarter and crush it flat on the table with the same hand. Right away bring the glass from under the table with the other hand. It looks like the glass passed through it.

Magical Ball of Paper

Present a small ball of paper to an audience member. Ask him to inspect it, then have it placed in the middle of your palm. Close your hand into a fist and open it again. The little ball disappears mysteriously. Close and open it again, and the pellet reappears much to the amusement of the audience. This can be done several times.

Secret: Before the presentation, stick a small piece of beeswax to the nail of your third finger. When closing your hand, grab the pellet with the third finger. When opening your hand again, show it at the proper angle so the paper ball is not shown.

Dirt in Eyes

The performer holds his eyes open while audience members dump buckets of dirt in them. He twitches for a second, then tears stream down his face, but his vision is fine.

Secret: The secret is to microwave the dirt to kill bacteria, and to use large contact lenses.

Dry as Water

Fill a fish bowl to the rim with water and ask someone from the audience to drop a coin in it. Dip your hand in the bowl. Retrieve the coin and show that your hand is still dry.

Secret: To perfect this stunt, sprinkle some Lycopodium powder on the surface of the water. This powder has no adhesives so it will keep the water away when you plunge your hand in.

Name the Card

Put a deck of cards in a large clear glass. Hold the glass at arm's length with the cards facing the audience. Mysteriously you are able to name each card before removing it from the deck.

Secret: You need a small mirror that you attach to a ring painted flesh color. A dental one is perfect. The ring/mirror is placed on the index of the hand that holds the glass, facing the front of the card.

This effect can also be done if you stick a small mirror on a piece of beeswax which is set on the tip of the index finger. Hold the finger in front of the card, so that the card is reflected in the mirror.

Valentine Trick

Place the queen of hearts on the back of your hand. Prop it up against a sewing needle that you hold behind the card between the index and third finger. People cannot see a sewing needle from three feet away, so it looks like the queen is balanced on the back of your hand.

One Good Apple

The performer has a bag of apples placed on a table. He explains to the audience that with intense concentration anyone can break an apple from stem to core with the bare hands.

The performer chooses an apple from the bag and gives a few to the volunteers who want to try. To show them he holds the apple straight up, putting one hand on one side, the other on the other side, and twists in opposite directions. While everybody is trying unsuccessfully, his apple breaks in half.

Secret: This feat is more than technique because the apple has been altered.

Prior to the demonstration, the performer pushed a long thin needle through the stem and into the core. By moving the needle from side to side and close to the skin it cuts the inside of the apple in half.

After this stunt, the performer can impress the audience even more. He can give a tricked apple to a volunteer explaining it only takes complete concentration to increase strength. When the volunteer succeeds, the performer's feat is proven.

Sawing a Woman in Half

A woman lies down in a long box, with her head and feet sticking out. The illusionist cuts the box in half through the middle, then separates the halves.

The head and feet are usually seen moving. When the two halves are brought back together, the woman comes out of the box unscathed.

Secret: Many methods have been used to create the effect. The secret of this famous illusion is that two women are used. The illustrations show their positions.

Sawing a Woman in Half Illustration:

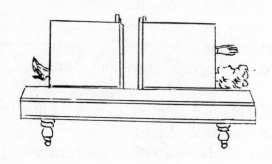

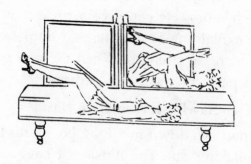

Mirror Mirage

Tell your audience that all mirrors can fool people. Here is an amusing stunt: have someone stand in front of a mirror with a magazine-size piece of paper and a pencil. Tell him to look at the paper through the mirror (not at the paper) and to draw a cross from corner to corner. You'll see that nobody is able to draw straight lines by looking through a mirror.

Secret: The reason is, since things in the mirror are reversed, the person draws under an unfamiliar circumstance.

Wooden Match Mysteries

#1: A wooden match can balance on a table surface.

Secret: While nobody is watching, moisten the end of the match, then press it hard on the table to make it stand straight. Make sure to wipe the excess moisture after the trick.

#2: Put nine wooden matches on the table. Ask your audience to form five triangles without breaking the matches.

See illustration for the answer.

#3: You can also balance a wooden match on top of your thumb.

Secret: To do this, bend the thumb and place the match in the crease of the knuckle. When raising the thumb, the match will stand straight.

#4: Place six wooden matches on the table and challenge a friend that half of eleven equals six.

Secret: Position the six matches so they form the Roman numeral XI. Now remove the bottom half (three matches) and what you have left is the Roman digit VI.

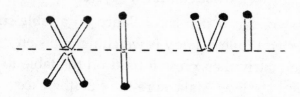

#5: Arrange four matches like a cross, ask someone to move only one to form a perfect square.

Secret: Gently move the bottom match down and a tiny square is formed right in the center of the crossed matches.

#6: Place two wooden matches on a dry surface as shown. Light one match and ask your audience how long it will take before the second match lights up. It's unlikely they will guess the second match won't ignite.

Secret: Once the first match is lit, it curls as it burns moving away from the head of the second match.

#7: Hold a burning wooden match between your index finger and thumb, at arm's length away from the body. Blow in the sleeve of the other arm. The flame of the match will go out.

Secret: While people are watching you blow in the sleeve, snap the third finger on the match.

Tens

Nine wooden matches are placed on a table. The performer asks his audience to change nine into ten. He places the matches in a way that will spell the number "TEN."

Now he takes four matches away, and the audience is asked to change five into ten.

Secret: The five matches form the number "10."

Three matches are taken away, the audience is asked to change two into ten.

Secret: One match is placed on top of the other to make the Roman number X.

For the finale, one of the two matches left on the table is discarded flamboyantly. The performer takes the other match and puts it in his left hand saying: "one into ten." He quickly closes his fingers on top of the match, then opens his left hand to show ten matches.

Secret: How he does it: he already has nine matches in his coat pocket. Right before the finale while finishing the last puzzle with his right hand, he palms the matches with his left. The flamboyant discard of the first match of the "X" distracts the audience for a fraction of a second. He quickly picks up the remaining match and puts it in his left hand which already has the other nine matches palmed.

Note: The performer who learns this trick well, will understand the importance of boldness for all manipulations.

Rising Arms

Here is an experiment based on a natural faculty of our body.

Ask someone to stand in a doorway (the narrower, the better) with arms at his sides. Then ask the volunteer to press the backs of his hands as hard as he can against the door frame while counting to twenty. Tell him to keep pushing with all his strength, then ask him to come forward. You'll see his arms rising.

Secret: This effect is caused by the continuing contraction of the muscles, as if the volunteer is still pressing his hands against the door frame.

This experiment often times is used as part of a hypnotic act.

Middle Eastern Strong Hold

Place on table a brass pot, a bag of white rice and a large kitchen knife. Each item is examined by the audience. Pour the rice inside the pot and dip the knife blade into the center of the rice. Lift the brass pot using the knife as a handle. Have everything passed around for another inspection.

Secret: To do this, the sides of the brass pot has been previously smeared with glue so that the rice adheres strongly to the pot which will hold the knife tight.

Rung Out

Ask two people from the audience to tie a rope to each one of your wrists, leaving a bit of rope in between them. While they're doing this you have a large metal ring examined by the audience. Sit behind a screen; after a few seconds, while still tied up, you show the ring dangling on the rope.

Secret: The secret is that you are hiding a second identical ring up in your rolled shirt sleeve. While behind the screen, hide the examined ring in your shirt or pants pocket, and let the concealed one roll down your arm.

Glowing Eyes

The performer asks a volunteer to sit on a chair. He explains that when the lights in the room are turned off, the volunteer will be able to see two glowing eyes staring at him.

Secret: When the lights are turned off, the performer puts pressure on the volunteer's closed eyelids with his thumbs and index fingers while explaining the feat, this will allow him to be more sensitive to vision in the dark. He keeps pressing on the lids for a while until the volunteer sees some fluorescent light on each corner of his eyes which is just an optic illusion caused by the pressure on the muscles and nerves. This is a subtle way to prepare him for the "glowing vision."

While the volunteer's eyes are still shut, the performer places two sticky fluorescent plastic rings to his own eyelids. Standing about five feet away from the volunteer, he closes his eyes and asks the volunteer to open his. The volunteer is astonished to see two fluorescent eyes staring at him.

Before the volunteer gets used to the darkness, the lights are turned on and the performer quickly opens his eyes which hides the fluorescent rings in his raised lids.

Rip a Phone Book with Your Hands

Place the bound side of the phone book on your thigh. Hold it with both hands firmly placed on each side. Make sure your fingers are curled over the pages for a strong hold. With equal pressure of the hands, bring the book together, and back, bending the pages. Do this a few times until a fold is formed in the center. When both sides are closer together, begin to tear by pulling up with one hand and tear down with the other. When the pages are bent, the tearing is much easier to do. What happens is you actually tear a few pages at a time, not the whole book at once.

The Easier Method: Put the phone book in a microwave for a few minutes to make it crispy and easy to tear.

Temperature Changing

First, take your temperature. Let everyone verify what it is. Then talk to your audience about mind over matter, willpower, etc. At the end of the lecture, take your temperature again and you will find that it's a few degrees higher.

Secret: Place a piece of strong soap under the left armpit, touching the skin.

Another version is to eat a small piece of strong soap, the size of a quarter, and drink plenty of hot tea. This version supposedly works better than the first one. I've never done it nor has anyone else I know, but it keeps showing up in different references.

Balancing Acts for the Dinner Table

#1: Hold a card between your index finger and your thumb. Place a wine glass on top of the card and let it balance.

Secret: You can do it by placing your index finger underneath the glass as shown.

#2: Here is another version: Hold a plate in your right hand, and place a glass on the rim. It looks like it balances on the edge.

Secret: You use your right thumb, extended upwards, to hold the glass.

#3: Place an uncooked egg in the middle of a plate and let it stand.

Secret: Beforehand put a teaspoon of salt in the middle of the plate, then press the egg on top. Carefully blow away the salt from around the egg. It will seem that the egg is standing by itself.

#4: Ask someone to arrange three glasses and three knives in a way that a fourth glass can be supported on top of the knives. The knives can be placed on top of the glasses, but cannot touch the table.

Secret: Interlock the blades and place the handles on the edges of the glasses. Once done, the fourth glass can be positioned on top of the triangle formed by the interlocking blades.

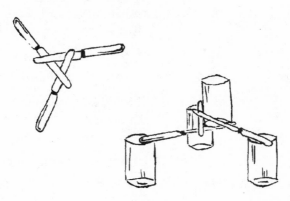

The Inflamed Sugar Cube

Challenge someone to set fire to a sugar cube so a flame is burning. That person will be unsuccessful, but you'll be able to do it with your "magical powers."

Secret: Give a sugar cube to a volunteer and ask him to set fire to it. It will burn and melt, but no flame will appear. Then ask him to give the sugar cube back to you. Have an ashtray nearby. Rest the melted half of the sugar lump on top of the ashes. Waste time fumbling with the lighter. Do not pay attention to the ashtray. While picking up the sugar cube press it hard on top of the ashes to get some to stick to the bottom. It will now easily catch on fire.

Pest Your Vest

Put a vest on in front of an audience. Then put your jacket on over it. Tell your audience that you will take the vest off while keeping the jacket on. To prove that you are not cheating, someone can hold one of your hands.

Secret: To start, use a screen (a tablecloth can be used). Have someone examine the vest and jacket. Then ask two people to hold the screen up. Have one of them hold one of your hands, then stand behind the screen, showing only your head and feet. Here are the moves to escape from the vest:

Unbutton the jacket with your free hand and have it slide off down your other arm. Then unbutton the vest and let it slide off down the same arm. Now reach to the jacket and pull it through the vest arm hole, making sure that it doesn't twist. Put your free arm through the jacket sleeve and button it up on the front. Bring the vest up and put it on top of the jacket which you also button. Before stepping out of the screen, tell your audience that you have not only taken the vest off while still wearing the jacket, you also put the vest back on, on top of the jacket!

They will think that you really did take it off and put it on again, but in fact it never comes off. To make this stunt look good, you have to move quickly. So practice with a friend.

Psychic Hand

A small compass is passed for examination and is placed anywhere a spectator designates. Performer now offers to demonstrate his magnetic power or control over natural laws by having the compass follow his finger. His arm is bared, so a concealed magnet is out of the question, yet the compass magically follows his finger. No amount of examination will disclose the performer's means of accomplishing this effect.

Secret: This effect is based on such simple means it may appear absurd. The only requirements are a common compass and for the performer it takes a good shock from a shocking machine. Those acquainted with electricity will subject themselves to one from a light socket which, however, is not suggested to the uninformed. Lay the compass down any place as long as it is not on metal. Now the motion of the finger placed near the compass will cause it to change direction and to follow the finger. This effect happens because the body retains a portion of the electricity after the shock, but spectators will search in vain for hidden magnets or pieces of metal. The effect is most uncanny.

Simple as this stunt is, it never fails to amuse and mystify, and is a delightful little stunt well away from the general run of tricks. Its simplicity should appeal to your magical taste.

The Human X-Ray Test

This simple yet effective experiment was first called to the attention of magicians by me, and while copied by others the true source of supply has been well hidden until now. The material cannot be obtained from drug stores as has been suggested, nor do many of the chemical supply houses carry the main ingredient. My source of supply was the Department of Organic Compounds of the Eastman Kodak Company, Rochester, New York.

Yes, this is a chemical effect, but so little known that it is quite startling. The performer makes his skin transparent, an effect quite equally unknown to the public as well as to magicians. Required is a great deal of showmanship and a dramatic presentation.

Concealed on the inside of the fakir's sleeve is a small container so hooked that it will be on the back side of the arm, away from the audience. The performer's palm is held toward the spectators. The effect is greater on this side of the arm, due to the number of blood vessels under the skin there.

As the shirt sleeve is rolled up, the opposite hand makes contact with the container, and quickly and indetectibly empties it into the palm. The band is then rubbed briskly over the arm. The shirt sleeve is given an extra roll; this hides the container and the arm can then be shown freely both back and front. Due to the distracting patter concerning his great power, the fakir will have time to indulge in the slight movement needed to empty the vial unnoticed. Even though this motion is simple, it requires showmanship. By all means leave this effect alone if you think you can entertain merely by rushing over to a pail, dipping your arm in and yelling, "Lookee!"

The chemical used is a mixture consisting of three parts salicylic methyl ester and one part benzyl benzoate.

Real Control of the Blood

Again simple, but it has fooled many doctors when presented by fakirs with any degree of showmanship. The hypnotist bares his subject's arms and calls attention to them. Both are the same color. After a few strokes, the blood is seen to leave and the arm is pure white. At command, the blood flows back.

Sitting naturally in a chair, note the color of the arms. Both naturally tinted. Now raise one arm above your head and hold it there while you slowly count to twenty-five. Now lower the arm and you will find it several shades lighter than the one that rests on the knees. So in the act of stroking the arm, it is held over the head and nature does the rest! Simple? Yes, but quite effective dressed with showmanship.

Metal Bending

Many mentalists claim that they can melt and bend metal objects like a spoon, fork or key by using their "extraordinary mental powers."

Fork Bending:

The mentalist places one fork on top of another, showing that they fit perfectly into one another. He asks a volunteer to hold a fork with one hand by the handle and the spike end with the other hand. The mentalist stares intently at the fork, "hypnotizing" it. He now asks the volunteer to reposition the two forks together as before. The spectator is baffled to witness a difference in the fork's shape.

Secret: What happens is while the volunteer is busy watching his own fork, the mentalist is bending the other one. With a good patter and misdirection, the volunteer doesn't know which of the forks was his and believes the fork he was holding had changed shape.

The One that Got Me

Just when we think we have it all figured out, something comes along to knock the life back into us. I have studied mentalism since the age of eight and thought I knew everything. What a mistake. One day in Spain, I was taken to a special demonstration that now makes me laugh every time I think about it.

There was a woman on stage sitting in a chair and holding a microphone with her back turned to the audience so there would be no chance of lip reading or hand signaling. From the audience the mentalist said that the lady in the chair was his wife, and that through strenuous mental experimentation he had learned to transfer his thoughts to her. Anybody could come up and whisper a word into his ear that he would transfer to his wife through concentration; and to prove it she would say the right word. And it worked every time. My brain was racing. She wasn't wearing an ear device; the people in the audience couldn't be plants because I had participated myself. How were they doing it?

Secret: After the demonstration, my friend told me that the mentalist was really a ventriloquist. Every time someone whispered a word to him, he'd say "OK." That would cue his wife to move her microphone up as though she were about to speak. When everyone turned their head to watch her answer the question, he'd change his voice and say the word into the microphone. His wife never said a word.

He literally talked to himself for a living.

GENIUS MIND

My Favorite Days

Give a calendar to an audience member and tell him to choose any month. Then with a pen ask him to circle any three days in a row. Tell him to add the three dates and give you the total. Right away you are able to guess which days he circled.

Secret: When the volunteer tells you the total, divide it by 3. The number you get is the second date of the three consecutive ones he circled.

Day Tripper

Hand a calendar to a volunteer, and while you're turning your back, ask him his favorite day of the week. Let's say it's Monday, tell him to go to any month and to circle three Mondays in a row. Ask him to add the three dates and to tell you the total. You'll then be able to guess the Mondays he chose.

Secret: To be able to call the right dates, mentally divide the total he gives you by 3. The result you get is the second Monday circled. To obtain the other two, subtract 7 to your result to get the first Monday, and add 7 to it to get the third Monday.

For example: The Mondays circled are the 4th, 11th and 18th. The total is 33. Divide 33 by 3 = 11. That is the middle Monday. 11 - 7 = 4 which is the first Monday circled; 11 + 7 = 18 which is the third Monday.

Here is a different version where you ask the volunteer to circle four consecutive Mondays. Tell him to add the four numbers and to give you the total. Again you can guess right away which ones he circled.

Secret: Subtract 14 from the total and divide the result by 4. The number you get is the second date circled. Then subtract 7 to get the first Monday, add 7 to get the third, and then add 14 to get the fourth Monday.

Let's say the number given you is 58:

58 - 14 = 44; 44 divided by 4 equals 11.

11th is the second Monday;

11 - 7 = 4; 4th is the first Monday;

11 + 7 = 18; 18th is the third Monday;

11 + 14 = 28; 28th is the fourth Monday.

I Know What You're Thinking

The performer says that he can read minds. He presents a phone book to a member of the audience and asks him to go to any page he likes and not to show it to him. Then the performer writes a number on a blackboard which he doesn't show to anyone. When he's ready, he asks the volunteer the page number he's chosen. It's the same one he's just written on the blackboard. For more effect the phone book is passed to another person. Again the performer guesses the same page number.

Secret: The performer is working with an assistant sitting in the audience. He chooses the first audience member sitting on the assistant's left side. When the phone book is passed around for the second time, it goes to the person sitting on the assistant's right side. In both cases, the assistant leans over and is able to see the page number which he communicates to the performer with a system they both know.

Psychic Object

You send your assistant to a different room. During his absence, the audience is required to choose an object in the room. Once done, call him back. Without a word and the help of a wand, point to the objects until he calls the one selected.

Secret: When you point to the chosen object, move your index finger a little to alert your assistant.

Sooth Sayer's Pride

In this stunt the performer is supposedly able to answer questions before looking at them.

He asks ten members of the audience to each write a question and their name on a piece of paper that they fold and put into a basket. The performer takes one at a time and brings it to his forehead and "telepathically" answers each question before reading it. He then verifies with the volunteers if his or her question has been properly answered.

Secret: This trick works by staying one question ahead of the audience.

The performer reaches into the basket and takes the first piece of paper that he brings to his forehead. After a deep "concentration," he seems to have difficulty to understand the question. He unfolds it, and says with surprise that no wonder he couldn't read it, it's written in an illegible scribble. Secretly he glances at the question.

He then crumples the paper and puts it in his pocket. Having seen the first question, it is now easy for him to do the whole act. He proceeds by taking a second folded paper out of the basket, holds it to his forehead, but instead of answering it, he actually answers the first one that he just put in his pocket. When he opens it to "verify" that he answered it right, he glances at the question that he will answer when he holds the next one to his forehead. He proceeds until all questions are answered.

Is the Person Alive or Dead?

Ten audience members are given a piece of paper on which they each write the name of a friend or a person unknown to the performer. One volunteer is chosen to write the name of a dead person, while others write the names of living people. The pieces of paper are dropped into a basket and mixed. By studying each name, the performer can reveal which one is the dead person.

Secret: It is easy to guess the name of the dead person because of the sharpness and lightness of the handwriting. Each person is given a soft lead point pencil, except for the one who writes the dead person's name; he gets the sharp point pencil.

Change in Pocket # 1

The performer says he will make a prediction and writes down how many coins a designated audience member has in his pocket. After the volunteer counts his coins, he is asked to say the number aloud.

The performer then shows him he has written the same number in his prediction.

The performer pretends to write on an index card with a pencil. Once he hears how many coins the volunteer has in his pocket, he secretly writes the exact number with his thumb tip.

*This is my favorite version of using a thumb tip writer (see *Chapter 2*).

Change in Pocket # 2

Here is another simple version to guess how many coins someone has in his pocket. This trick can be done while your back is turned to the audience.

Ask a volunteer to write any number on a piece of paper and not to let you see it. Let's say he chose 10. Tell him to multiply it by 2 (10 X 2 = 20), and to then add 8 (20 + 8 = 28) and now to divide that number by 2 (28 divided by 2 = 14). Then tell him to subtract the original number from the final result (in our example 14 - 10 = 4).

To finish, tell him to add it to the number of coins he has in his pocket (let's say he has 5 coins so 5 + 4 = 9). Ask him the total (in this case it is 9). When the volunteer tells you what it is, always mentally subtract 4 from it (in our example 9 - 4 = 5).

The number you get (in our example 5) is the number of coins he has in his pocket.

The Shoes Say it All

The performer brings five or six people onstage. A folded bandana is put over his eyes. He asks one volunteer at a time to come towards him and to place a personal object in the palm of his extended hand. Once they've all done it, the performer, after removing the handkerchief, will be able to identify the owner of each object.

Secret: The secret is to be able to see the shoes of the person who hands over an object. This can be done easily with the blindfold trick listed under *Devices And Sleights for Deception.*

Two Heads Equal One

There are "super natural power" seminars that use tricks. The meeting starts off with a discussion about how everyone should stay on the same page.

Two volunteers are brought up. One is told to leave the room. The speaker has two 3x5 white index cards with a circle drawn on them and a dot in the middle. He hands one to the volunteer and asks him to stare at the dot, and to think of a number.

Let's say he chooses number 54. The speaker asks him to announce the number and to write it over the dot but inside the circle. While the volunteer is doing this, the speaker uses his thumbnail to secretly indent the same number over the dot on the other card. After the person has written the number, he is instructed to put the card in his pocket.

When the secluded volunteer comes back onstage, he is told to stare at the dot until a number appears (notice instructions have been changed slightly because the speaker wants him to see the indentation). If he has a hard time seeing, the speaker shifts him around a little so the light hits at the right angle. He then tells him to write the number down. After he falls for it, and they always do, the volunteers are told to exchange their slips of paper and to read each other's number aloud. They are both the same.

Never a Loser

Get two people from the audience and challenge them to a gamble in which they cannot lose. You have three envelopes of the same size, one ten dollar bill and two scraps of paper the same size as the ten dollar bill. The bill and the two pieces of paper are folded and each placed in an envelope. The envelopes are mixed, and you and each of the two audience members get one. Whoever gets the ten dollar bill gets to keep it. Because of your magical power, it seems that you always get the money.

Secret: Here's how it's done: Glue a small piece of pencil lead to the ten dollar bill. Hide it by holding it with your thumb. Tell the volunteers to fold the pieces of paper in half by demonstrating with the bill. Then hand the folded bill to one of them. Turn your back and ask him to put the money and each of the two pieces of paper in different envelopes. Ask him to seal them and to place them back on the table. You mix them up and ask spectator # 1 to pick one. Take it and feel it.

If he took the one with the money, tell him that he picked yours, then proceed by asking both of them which envelope they want for themselves. If spectator #1 didn't pick the one with the money, then let him have the envelope he chose.

Now ask spectator #2 to pick one envelope. You do the same as above, if he chooses a regular one, give it to him; if he chooses the one with the money, keep it and tell him he picked it for you.

In every case, you will always be the winner. (See the section *The Sure Bet*).

I Know the Music Playing in Your Head!

I saw this mentalist in Belgium last year during the Ghent Festival who had a little act that was so sweet I can't wait to describe it for you.

The performer had ten cassette tapes that all looked the same because there were no markings. He demonstrated that each one had a different type of music by playing a little from each one Rock N' Roll, Violin Solo, Jazz, Rumba, Folk, Sinatra, Spiritual, Opera, Sousa March, and Reggae. When finished, he'd mix them all up and put them in a bag which was handed to an audience member. He'd write something on a piece of paper and ask the volunteer to reach in and pick out any cassette. The one he picked was the violin solo. He asked the volunteer to read the prediction which said "Violin Solo."

Secret: No one caught it but me. Each cassette had ten seconds of different style of music, but the rest of it was the violin solo.

Magazine, Anyone?

For this "telepathy" trick take six Newsweek magazines. Replace the covers of five of them with covers from other editions. Now they look like different issues, but the inside pages are all the same.

First, the performer shows the six "different" magazines to the audience and asks a volunteer to pick one. The performer walks back to the table and nonchalantly puts four magazines down and keeps one to show the volunteer what he has to do.

He says, "pick any page and say out loud which one you chose." The volunteer is asked to look at the page very carefully, but not to show it to anybody.

Meanwhile the performer secretly scans the same page in his magazine paying attention to titles, pictures, and most of all the last word before putting it down. He asks the volunteer to concentrate on his page as hard as he can. He explains that telepathically he can recreate the page on the chalkboard. The performer slowly does a rough sketch and writes the final word that was on the page. The volunteer is then asked to verify the sketch and last word, which of course represents his page.

Pin City

Some people who say they can predict your future will give a public demonstration to prove it. Everyone is guided to a room with a 2 X 3 foot map of the United States that is attached to a cork board hanging on the wall. The fortune teller writes something on a piece of paper, puts it in an envelope, seals it and asks a volunteer from the audience to put it in his pocket. He then puts a blind fold on the volunteer and places him in front of the map. He hands the volunteer a pin and tells him to wave his arm around in circles and push the pin anywhere into the map.

After he has done this, the blind fold is taken off and the volunteer is instructed to call out the name of the city that is closest to the pin. He's then told to take the envelope from his pocket, open it and read the paper. It is the same city that is stuck with the pin.

Secret: This is not a true prediction, it's a trick. The fortune teller seats everybody five to ten feet away from the map because there is already a pin in it, but you can't see it from that distance. The only one that has a chance of seeing it is the volunteer, that's why he's blindfolded.

The reason the fortune teller places the blind folded volunteer directly in front of the map is to block the audience's view of where he is placing the pin. The fortune teller takes a flashlight and boldly shines it on his pre-placed pin and tells the volunteer to take off the mask.

While the audience watches the pin and the volunteer takes off the mask, our friendly fortune teller casually leans against the part of the map with the other pin and palms it. The volunteer is then asked to name the city closest to the pin and it just happens to be the same city written in the envelope.

Memory of an Elephant

Have a person list 30 objects numbered from 1-30. Once done, the volunteer gives you the list which you are allowed to study and memorize for one minute. When you hand the list back, you prove your memory skill by recalling each object in order.

Then the volunteer is instructed to mention any of the numbers at random and you are able to recall the objects listed for that number. The volunteer can also mention any of the thirty objects, and you are able to recall its given number.

The Human Computer:

To do this, memorize 30 numbers with keywords that can trigger an action. See my codes below. Let's start with number 1.

I use the key word "Gun" for number 1 because it rhymes making it easier to remember. For the action I picture the object getting shot.

Let's say the volunteer lists "book" as the object for number 1. Since I memorized 1 = Gun, I picture the book getting shot by a gun as the action that triggers the memory. When I am asked to recall number

1, I think of "Gun," and immediately remember the book getting shot. If the person names the object and says "book," a book getting shot comes to my memory which equals "Gun." Gun = 1.

Once a mental picture for an action is locked in for a number, quickly go to the next object until you've completed the person's list. With a little practice, images will pop into your head rapidly making you a human computer.

Below you'll find a list for 30 words that I think are best. To start, practice with ten and work up as you get comfortable. Stick with the formula.

Key Words:

Number One = Gun
The action is:
Shooting the object with a gun.

Number Two = Blue
The action is:
Painting the object blue with a brush.

Number Three = Key
The action is:
Holding the object in a key ring.

Number Four = Flower
The action is:
Imagine smelling the object as if it were a flower.

Number Five = Dry
The action is:
Using a blow dryer on the object.

Number Six = Sea
The action is:
The object is floating in the sea.

Number Seven = Heaven
The action is:
An angel is carrying the object to Heaven.

Number Eight = Crate
The action is:
Placing the object into a big crate.

Number Nine = Pine
The action is:
The object is balanced on a pine cone.

Number Ten = Pen
The action is:
Writing on the object with a pen.

Number Eleven = Hell
The action is:
Picture the Devil holding the object stuck on its pitch fork.

Number Twelve = Self
The action is:
Carrying the object on myself.

Number Thirteen = Drinking
The action is:
Drinking a glass of water that contains the object.

Number Fourteen = Flirting
The action is:
Two people are kissing.

Number Fifteen = Lifting
The action is:
Lifting the object with my finger.

Number Sixteen = Sweet Sixteen
The action is:
The object is immersed in honey.

Number Seventeen = Pouring
The action is:
The object keeps pouring out of a pitcher.

Number Eighteen = Eating
The action is:
Eating the object.

Number Nineteen = Hammering
The action is:
A hammer keeps smashing the object.

Number Twenty = Penny
The action is:
A penny is standing on top of the object.

Number Twenty-One = Sun
The action is:
Covering the object with sun tan lotion.

Number Twenty-two = Shoe
The action is:
Putting the object into a shoe.

Number Twenty-Three = Flea
The action is:
A flea is hopping on the object.

Number Twenty-Four = Saw
The action is:
Sawing the object.

Number Twenty-Five = Beehive
The action is:
Bees are buzzing around the object.

Number Twenty-Six = Trick
The action is:
Holding a top hat where the object is produced from.

Number Twenty-Seven = Shaven
The action is:
Shaving the object with an electric shaver or razor, whichever you prefer.

Number Twenty-Eight = Gate
The action is:
The object is standing in front of an iron gate.

Number Twenty-Nine = On the Line
The action is:
Placing the object parallel to a line.

Number Thirty = Dirty
The action is:
Washing the object since it's dirty.

Note: It is not only a very entertaining stunt, it is also a skill that trains the mind and can be used in everyday life.

Brain Eraser # One

After doing the feat of recalling the objects that a person has given you (see *Memory of an Elephant*), tell him that you can erase all objects from your mind except for one.

Ask him to randomly cross out each object and to say loudly at the same time what it is. For example: "I'm crossing out the number six, I'm crossing out the number ten, I'm crossing out the number three," etc, until one number is left. Immediately you can recall the exact item that corresponds to the remaining number.

Secret: When the volunteer crosses out the objects, add the numbers together in your head. Once all 29 numbers are called out, subtract the total from 465. The number you get will be the only one left.

When working with thirty objects, know that if you add the numbers together you get a total of 465. If you are working with twenty objects, the total of these numbers is 210. If you are working with ten objects, the total is 55.

Brain Eraser # Two

This one works only with ten objects. Turn your back to the audience and hang your arms at your sides. Have your fingers touch your legs and imagine that each one represents the numbers between 1 and 10.

When the audience member calls out the numbers, lift the corresponding fingers, until one is left touching the leg. The corresponding number will be the object left out on the list (*see Memory of an Elephant*).

At the Risk of Bodily Harm...

Tough Man with Lockjaw

Lifting and swinging a person with your teeth can be entertaining, or it can get you thrown in jail. It's a good one if you're trying to entertain.

Neck muscles are much stronger than people think, especially if they are exercised. The lifting is easy. The secret is knowing that it can't be done with teeth. It can only be done with the pressure of a mouth piece going against the upper concave part of your mouth.

Take a 2 1/2 x 3 1/2 foot piece of canvas and attach a small chain to each corner. The four chains are held together with a longer one attached to a hook that you have wrapped with leather for your mouthpiece. Glue enough leather to fit snugly into your mouth.

Now tell the volunteer to lie down on the canvas and make sure that he's well balanced. When ready to lift, bend your knees. Put pressure on your upper legs with your hands as you straighten your legs and start lifting.

One-Finger Lift

Very few people know that they can lift more weight with one finger than they can with both hands.

Place a heavy weight (it could be a block of steel) between your legs. Attach a hook to the weight where you'll lift from. Put the third finger of the lifting hand through a ring that is attached to the hook. The finger must fit tightly and snugly. Make sure to get a good hold when curling it around the ring. Bend the knees and place the free hand on one knee and keep the lifting arm straight the entire time. Start the lifting by straightening the legs and putting more pressure with the hand on the knee.

This stunt can be achieved easily with practice. Many men can lift over 400 pounds. When doing it for the first time, lift a small amount of weight and work your way up.

Run-Over Fun

A man lies on the ground while a car is driven over his body. After the stunt, he comes out unharmed.

Secret: There is only one way to do it semi-safely. The man lies between two ramps placed at the thighs, and one inch shorter than his body while flattened to the ground. When the car drives up the ramp and the front wheels are on his body, he doesn't feel it because all the weight has been shifted to the lower back wheels. When the front wheels have passed over him, the car is now pointing down on the other side of the ramp, shifting the weight to the hood and making the weight of the back wheels pain-free as well.

Sword Swallowing

This is a fine example of how bodies can be altered, and how you can trick the natural order. Sword swallowers tickle their gag reflexes seven times a day for three years until they stop gagging. Once the reflex no longer responds, they can shove a sword down the esophagus into the stomach effortlessly.

To tickle the reflex they typically start by sticking a finger down their throat, until they just about throw up. They do it repeatedly until they can slide their finger down with no response. After that, they use a dull fencing sword, pushing it down as far as they can, gradually getting it down farther and farther. After years the body is modified, and once it stops responding to foreign intruders such as swords, the skill is achieved.

Unfortunately some people buy fake swords that collapse when they're pushed in. Widespread use of this trick dims the lustre of the true masters.

Hold a Man Overhead with One Hand

This one will sure bring a round of applause. Tell your audience that you can hold someone over your head with just one hand.

Pick someone and make him stand up on a chair. Attach a belt or a strong rope securely under his arms at his armpits. With your right hand, grab the belt in the middle of the chest area. While raising your arm straight, bend your knees and turn your back to him at the same time. Now straighten your legs and lift the person off the chair. Let his body rest on your back. When walking around, you carry him on your back more than with your arm. But since your legs are stronger than your arms, they're really what lift the person. Do not allow your arm to bend at any time.

To do this stunt successfully, start by lifting a lightweight person. Practice for a while, and soon you will be able to dance around while holding the person with one hand.

Magical Weight Gain

Even a small person cannot be lifted by a strong man if she puts pressure to the side of his neck with her right forefinger, and pressure on top of his right wrist with her left hand.

Suspended Animation

Among the Todas tribe in the Nilgiri Hills of South India, a spectacular stunt is performed. They pack both nostrils and mouth with cotton, then on top of all this pour sand. Yet they remain this way for hours and still live!

Secret: When putting cotton in the mouth the tongue is curved back and thus prevents the complete blocking of the throat. The nostrils are only lightly packed with cotton and breathing is lightly done through the nose since the subject is supposed to enter into a trance. Little air is needed and thus obtained. The sand is packed only into the mouth.

Hold Fire with Your Hands

While holding a fire eating dinner torch, pass your hand over it and squeeze it carefully between your fingers. Some of the flaming fluid will drip in your hand giving an illusion that you're holding fire in the palm. To cut the chances of getting burned, hold your arm straight out with the palm up and flat. Remember to keep the fingers together.

The flame will extinguish as soon as the fluid evaporates.

Eating Red Hot Pepper

Before working this effect, oil your mouth and tongue well with pure olive oil. The rest is simple. You can hold the hottest pepper on your tongue with no ill effect. You can eat pepper like ice cream.

Note: It is interesting to note here that a recent news report told of a child dying because his mother forced him to eat pepper for misbehaving. Child died of asphyxiation. Mother thought the punishment would be mild.

Walking on Hot Coals

Certain self-help groups have been using this feat as the ultimate confidence booster. Fact is, this is one of the easiest of all the Hindu, yogi and fakir stunts. Just let the coals heat up so only the cores are burning and there is a lot of ashes around them. They are measured out, so it takes five steps or less to get across them. Coal walkers must move rapidly and be off the coals within seven seconds or the heat will register.

A cheater alternative: some use volcanic rock, which doesn't retain as much heat as coals and actually looks more impressive to the uninitiated.

Human Bench

This stunt is not for the weak, but anybody who has a strong body can do it.

Sit on the floor, place your arms straight behind you and raise your knees. Then lift your body so that it is supported by your hands and feet which are flat on the floor. Make sure that your body is parallel to the floor and that your arms and legs are perpendicular to it.

Hold this position firmly. Then have an assistant balance a long flat board across the knees. Ask six people to sit on the piece of wood, three on each side. Once it is done, ask them to lift their feet from the floor so that the whole weight is supported by only your body.

Eating a Glass Light Bulb

Light bulb glass is usually very thin, although I've

been in some countries where it's quite thick, which causes a bit of a problem and indigestion. Glass eaters chew softly to avoid the glass from popping on their gums and tongue, creating cuts. They also eat a banana before and after the stunt to ameliorate the effect of digesting Edison's invention.

After chewing the shards gently down to small fragments, the glass eater chews with more authority. The goal is to try to reduce the glass back into sand. Once the shards are particle-sized, he swallows with little danger.

This stunt can pose a problem for those with cavities or sensitive teeth because it strips the enamel.

Fire-Eating

Half of this act is making the torches. Fire eaters take cotton strings off a mop, tighten them into a ball with copper wire, and affix the ball around the end of a coat hanger. The ball is then squirted with lighter fluid.

Once the torch is lit, fire eaters lick their lips to make sure the mouth is moist. They arch their head back as far as it can go, so that the flames brought towards their mouth are going upward. They never breathe in during this act.

The key is to breathe out slowly enough so as not to put the flames out. They continue breathing slowly out of their mouth as the fire is lowered past their lips and into their oral cavity. They give one last puff of air and close their lips extinguishing it in the process.

Flaming Banana

Pour a little alcohol in a bowl and light a match to it. Peel a banana and dip one end into the alcohol. Bring the flaming banana to your mouth and eat it bit by bit.

*This stunt is done the same way as fire eating. Wet your lips and mouth with saliva, hold your head back (at about 75 degrees) so that the fire doesn't burn the roof of your mouth. Exhale as you close your mouth on the banana.

Hammer a Nail with Your Hand

Wrap the top of a ten-penny nail very heavily with a handkerchief so that it forms a ball in the palm of your hand. The success depends on how the wrapping of the cloth is done. It gives you a better grip and will protect you from getting hurt. Position the nail very tight between the index and third finger.

Raise your hand and with all your strength, slam the nail straight into the board. The nail has to hit the board straight or you'll fail the feat. Start by using a thin board; as you succeed use a thicker one. But always use soft wood. The audience won't be able to tell the difference.

Can't Break Away

1: Fold your arms high on the chest and stand very straight with your feet steady and apart for balance. A towel is attached to each upper-arm. Ask two men to take position on each side of you and tell them to separate your arms from your chest by pulling the towels. You'll see they cannot do it.

Secret: To do this stunt, make sure they pull your upper arms steadily with no quick jerks, and they stay away from the elbows or you will lose your balance.

You can do the same stunt without the towels; instead have the men try to pull your upper arms apart.

2: Bend your arms in front of your chest in a way that the tips of both index fingers are touching. Ask a person to stand in front of you and to hold your right wrist with his left hand, and your left wrist with his right hand. Now challenge him to separate your fingers without quick jerks. No matter how much effort he uses, he won't be able to pull them apart.

Secret: The secret lies in the fact that you can resist the pull better than him. The only way he can separate them is if he pulls one hand up and the other down.

Hot Coal Diet

Build a fire of charcoal, then add some soft pieces of pine that are the same size. Once blackened, put a fork in one of them (that's how they will be recognized you can't put a fork through the burned charcoal). Moisten your mouth with saliva and put the burning piece on a very wet tongue. The burned pine won't be as hot as burned charcoal.

This can also be done by using burnt cottonballs that have been dipped in alcohol. You can also pick them up with a fork.

Light a Cigarette in Your Mouth

Use a non-filter cigarette. Place a lighted match underneath one end with the flame away from the end.

Toss your head back and bring the flaming match and cigarette inside your open mouth. A few seconds later, the flame is out, but the cigarette is lit.

Secret: When bringing the match and cigarette to the mouth, blow very gently toward the cigarette. It will cause the flame to go toward the cigarette's end and to light it.

Two Strong Fists

Ask a volunteer to place one of his fists on top of the other. Now you tell him that you can push them apart with only two index fingers.

Secret: Stand in front of him with your hands closed but leaving both index fingers free. Simultaneously, strike his top fist with your right index finger, and the bottom one with your left index finger. It will work every time.

Now if someone challenges you with the same feat, be prepared to beat him. Secretly place the thumb of the bottom fist inside the upper fist. No matter how much force he uses to separate them with his index fingers, they will never be strong enough.

Five-Finger Discount

A heavy person can easily be lifted with five fingers. No devices are used for this feat.

Place the volunteer in the middle of the room. Have one person position his index under the volunteer's chin, a second puts one index under the right foot, a third puts one index under the left foot, a fourth and fifth put an index under each armpit.

When ready, they lift the volunteer simultaneously which distributes the weight. If the volunteer is 150 pounds, each person is only responsible for lifting 30 pounds.

Note: *Be careful with what you do with this information, some of it may be outdated or slightly incorrect.*

FEATS
OF TORTURE

One of the first books I ever read that got me interested in secrets of the strange was Feats of Torture, *written by Joseph Ovette. This book is now out of print, but it was so influential to me that I've included his experiences in this chapter. I've also added a few experiences of my own.*

Branding Oneself with a Hot Iron

I t will be well to mention that the main qualities in any of these feats are nerve and pure guts, and plenty of both. That is putting it plain. Only a person with plenty of nerve should consider tackling this type of work.

All you need here is a common electric soldering iron properly connected and working, and your arms bared. Hold the iron in your right hand and gently but lightly place the iron on the skin, searing it.

IT WILL BURN, but not much, if the branding is lightly done. Be sure the iron is HOT. An added effect can be had by smearing the spot to be branded with Vaseline. Then when the iron touches the arm it will cause a hissing sound. This lessens the danger of burning, but watch for persons who faint!

Needle Jabbing

Use long surgical needles and be sure they are sterilized well. Extend your arm. Tell someone to grasp a bunch of skin and to pull it up. With the needle in your right hand jab it through the skin. The only pain you will experience will be a slight sting. Several needles can be so inserted.

Draw out the needle slowly and the blood will not flow and thus you can also demonstrate the stoppage of the blood. The needles can also be run through the cheek, from cheek to cheek, or through the loose skin under the neck.

Note: A firm pressure before inserting the needle practically anesthetizes the area. This is known as "pressure anesthesia," and is frequently used by dentists before inserting their needle. Only a sharp sting is felt.

Fangs of Lucifer

A variation of the above was marketed by me as the Fangs of Lucifer. In this the fakir demonstrates his ability to render his body immune to common place injuries. Long heated needles are deliberately thrust through various parts of the body and permitted to cool. They are then withdrawn and no blood flows from the wounds, nor is there any sign of pain.

Principle and application are the same as the preceding torture. But since the explanations given are fuller we will expand them here. No preparation is needed, although rubbing the arm with a strong salt solution before the test will prove beneficial. Warm needles. That is, heat them, but do not get them red hot since that may blunt the points. Insert needles with a firm, steady push, either fakir or an assistant holding up the flesh (pressure anesthesia).

A slight pain will be experienced as the needle goes through; after that no pain with the possible exception of a throbbing due to the excessive heat of the needle. Several needles may be inserted, then permitted to cool. In drawing these out, do so quickly, since the needles will tend to stick as the flesh may be seared or the cooling blood coagulate.

To finish, dab the punctures with peroxide or iodine and upon retiring, place a dab of carbolated Vaseline on the wounds. In a couple of days all signs of the experiment will disappear.

In using surgical needles, you will find them very thin, the thinner the better, and sharp. The genuine fakir uses hatpins which, by the way, are not very sharp nor strong. You, though, should sterilize your needles, the heat in most cases being ample.

There are some who, to make the effect more grue-
some, break the needles off or suspend weight from
their ends. A dab of Vaseline can add to the effect
since it will hiss and sear like burning flesh when
touched with the hot needle. This is not a pleasant
sight or effect, to be sure, but there are many who
have found that they can sit and grin and shove
needles into their skin at will.

The Trap Trick

This has been a very popular effect with magicians
and still is because it presents such an unusual effect.

The performer sets a steel trap and then places
his finger in it to set it off, the jaws crashing against
his finger but no damage is done. The type of trap to
use is one of those steel double-jawed traps generally used for catching foxes and other wild game.
These have a round pan and are easily set.

Do not use a rat trap. That is the kind that breaks
a rat's neck; whereas this style of trap is made to
hold the animal and not to kill.

With the trap set, extend your finger and place it
straight down on the pan and release the latter. The
trap will spring and the jaws come against the finger
at the joint near the knuckle. There will be no pain,
just a sharp rap. Traps, as stated above, are made to
hold the animal, and this fact is not generally known.
The spectators see the jaws crash and they will think
your finger is gone.

Try it with a stick at first and then a heavy glove
if nervous or if it is necessary to work up courage

first. *Don't try to jerk the finger out or put it in sideways.* Do it *slowly* and quite deliberately, for you will soon learn there is no harm to this feat if properly done.

Drinking Acid

The fakir exhibits a small whiskey glass and a bottle of carbolic acid, which may be examined. He next fills the glass and drinks it, much to the amazement of the audience.

Secret: The fact that a small whiskey glass is used serves to convince the audience that the acid is deadly, but fakir really *drinks only water.* The glass is a special glass, a little taller than usual with a mirror division. Mirror is firmly cemented in. The side into which the acid is poured further connects with a double bottom hidden by a design in the glass or a band painted on. Thus the acid poured into the glass runs into the secret compartment and remains there even when the glass is tilted to pour the water out. The water side is filled, the water being suitably colored if necessary to match the acid.

The glass is picked up and shown apparently empty and filled with acid. Hand covers most of this action and glass is reversed in the process showing now a "full" glass.The acid is placed back on the table and the fingers slid down to reveal the "full" glass held at fingertips. After some dramatic display, glass is lifted to lips and "emptied," the mouth being held wide open so "acid" will not splash.

Editor's note: Carbolic acid (phenol) is a deadly caustic, and even a spilled drop or two proves quite

painful. The handling of such materials even by the
fakir, or examination of same by the audience, is cer-
tainly not to be recommended.

Putting Fingers in Hot Lead

This remarkable test outclasses many stunts of the
fakirs. A pot of genuine molten lead is exhibited and
performer asks audience to choose a finger from his
hand that he shall insert in same. He places this finger into the hot lead and withdraws it without seem-
ing ill effect.

Secret: This feat requires great *care* and *greater nerve*.
The hands must be devoid of *all* moisture. They *must*
be perfectly dry. This can be done by "washing" the
hands with dry sand. Anything that will tend to dry
the hands will help, for the chief thing to remember
and have is *dry hands*. The hands may be "fire-
proofed" if desired, but this is not necessary.

When putting the finger in the lead, it is placed
in straight and withdrawn in the same direction. Motion is not swift nor too slow but deliberate. The hot
lead will not have time to burn, and since it will roll
off a dry surface it cannot cling and inflict injury. To
the audience this is convincing demonstration of su-
perhuman power (and nerve).

Bar Through Tongue

An Italian by the name of Frankroy, posing as an
Asian, presented the following in New York. Playing
side shows and stores, he tells that the effect is old
in his own country although seldom seen elsewhere.

A steel hook is pushed through his tongue. A large vase full of water, supposedly weighing five hundred pounds is suspended from the hook and the performer whirls around with all this dangling from his tongue.

Secret: The hook is curved like the old knife through the arm. It is switched for the genuine hook under cover of cleaning the same. The fake hoop loops around the tongue and the teeth hold the brace. The vase has a small capacity because of a false partition, hence holds much less water than supposed. It is made of light hammered brass and though appearing heavy is really light.

Piercing the Tongue

The Hindu extends his tongue and proceeds to shove a long needle right through. In some cases a button is even sewed on!

Secret: A false tongue is made of flesh-colored rubber, and don't think that this cannot be most convincing. Someday you will be fooled by this! This extra tongue is concealed between cheek and teeth, then mouth may be opened and shown "empty." Mouth is closed and then the tongue is apparently stuck out and the demonstration proceeds. The rest is easy. Of course, with all these demonstrations, suitable costuming and patter helps "sell" the trick.

Pierced Weight-Lifting

Anyone who wants his or her body parts pierced for weight lifting should use an experienced piercer. Those who pierce their tongue discover that it thickens, making eating or talking difficult for weeks. Nipples are pretty normal; ears are fine.

Practitioners must keep an object inserted so the holes don't close. They add large gauged jewelry to widen the holes in the same way that Africans do. The holes are gradually stretched larger and larger. Once the holes are a size that can take hooks, they attach the hooks to a light chain and to objects they want to lift.

The weightlifter's goal is to callous the areas that take the weight. So they start with something small and work their way up to heavier objects. As all pierced weightlifters can tell you, they put up with large amounts of discomfort for many years to perfect their act.

Buried Alive

Of the many means for performing this, the following is the best.

A grave is dug and a box placed in. The performer gets in and places a rubber hood over his head and the box is covered. Just before this, a long cane pole with a flag on the upper end is stuck in the box. This can be announced as a mark of identification or a means of signaling. The entire grave and box is now covered.

The secret of the entire thing rests in the cane pole. This is hollow and the performer, getting his mouth into the bottom end, breathes the air freely. Not one in a thousand will suspect the pole as it is too tall for a spectator to see the end and is seemingly serving a useful purpose. One can stay underground by this method quite indefinitely. This is much less dangerous than other methods.

The Human Fountain

Another novelty seen was Mantado. He stands in a night club with streams of water spurting from the palms of his hands and from his feet. He is billed as the "Human Fountain." You can look at his hands and feet and actually see the water shooting forth.

Mantado has had operations performed to accomplish this. Doctors have pierced his palms and feet and inserted silver tubes. To these, rubber tubes are attached and strapped to his arms and legs where they are hidden. They run to a hidden water supply. This is quite an astonishing effect since the water is permitted to run for hours.

Another freak, named Jo-Gods, has created considerable comment among doctors. He does the usual fakir stuff, then takes out his eye for examination! The eye is really blind and still connected to the optic nerves, etc. A most nauseating performance, and as one has remarked, "What won't a person do to keep from working?"

Human Radio Feature

A wonderful advertising stunt using the needle jabbing test with it. This is intended for window or lobby work in a theater or store. Seat yourself in a chair with a loud speaker on one side and the receiving set on the other. Insert a needle in the left arm and one in the right. Connect the wire from the receiving set to one needle and the speaker wire to the other. Now have the radio tuned in. The music passes through the body. This is wonderful bally effect, and no harm can result from this. It is best not to use too powerful a set.

Human Pincushion

The maxim here is "If you can pinch an inch of skin, you can stick a pin through." Professional pincushions typically ram needles and skewers through their arms, legs, throats, chests, cheeks and eyebrows anywhere they can lift extra skin. The keys are: do not ram needles through vein and capillary systems; and when pulling needles out, pull slowly, giving any blood that may have formed time to coagulate.

Pincushions typically start with pins, then gradually work their way up to skewers. They develop sweet spots and can eliminate the original discomfort associated with this act.

BAR BETS/
IMPRESS YOUR FRIENDS
AND WIN FREE DRINKS

Knife in a Glass

A bartender friend of mine told me that one time this guy walked in, took out his knife and said: "I want to show you something cool." He stuck the knife gently into the ceiling right above the bar, then asked for a glass of water and said: "I bet I can make that knife fall out of the ceiling and into this glass without breaking it."

He took the glass and raised it up to the knife and got the handle wet. He placed the glass exactlywhere the drip from the knife landed on the bar. Then he lifted a bar stool and slammed it onto the floor. The vibration freed the knife from the ceiling, and because the handle is the heavy end, it dropped straight down into the glass without breaking it.

Cheesy Bar Bet

A guy with a half-pound of cheese walked into a bar and said: "I can eat this half-pound of cheese before any of you can finish your beer." Everyone gulped their beer down and waited for him to finish the cheese. After he chewed the last morsel, he went around and cocked each drinker's beer glass so that gravity pooled the remaining drops, and said: "I won. You still have beer to finish."

Secret: The bottom of a beer glass is a bar owner trick in itself. It works two ways:

One: A person needs to buy more beer to get to his personal cut off-line.

Two: When a person has decided to get one more drink, he psychologically expects the last gulp. After futilely tipping the glass a couple of times, the old alcohol devil whispers to the brain: "Get another one."

Drunk and Acrobatic

This one's great to get free drinks at a bar: Bet anybody that you can walk on your hands for a distance of 20 feet.

Secret: Once the challenge is called, bend over, put your hands underneath your feet, and start walking on your hands!

Rising Salt Shaker

This could be done at the dinner table without much preparation. Hold your fingers straight above a salt shaker. A few seconds later, it appears that the shaker is rising from the table by your finger tips.

Secret: While holding your fingers at the top of the shaker, insert a toothpick through one of the holes and hold it between your fingers. The salt shaker should be full; it's more impressive and the toothpick gets a better grip.

Unusual Fireworks

Light a candle and spray the juice of an orange peel towards the flame; it will produce unusual fireworks.

A Spoonful of Fire

Pour a little bit of gasoline in the bottom of a bowl and light a match to it. Dip a spoon into the bowl until it catches fire. Then bring the flaming spoon to your mouth and swallow. People will believe that you swallowed burning gasoline.

Secret: You actually swallow nothing.

Make sure your lips are wet. While closing your mouth around the spoon, you gently blow the flame out. You then pretend to swallow. Remember to never breathe in when doing a fire stunt.

Fire Bar Bet

Place a piece of paper on top of a glass, and a dime on top of the paper. Challenge your friends to make the dime fall inside the glass without touching the paper.

Secret: To do this, light a match, and hold it close to the piece of paper without touching it. The heat will ignite the paper. Once it is burned, the dime will fall into the glass.

Deck of Cards Torn in Half

Place the left half of the 52 card deck on the palm of the left hand, the left thumb resting on the lower left side of the deck and the four fingers grasping it tightly by the bottom. The right hand holds the other side of the deck in a reverse position, the right thumb resting on the upper right side. Hold them firmly and bend them in the middle to weaken them. Then twist the hands in opposite directions, right hand to the right and left hand to the left, like screwing the cap off a jar. Do it a few times and you will notice the cards tearing in the middle. Do this until they are completely torn apart.

At first you might want to rest the left hand on one knee for support when bending and twisting the deck. After some practice you won't need to use the knee. Also, the first few times you might want to start with less cards, and add more as you go.

Some people are so good at this they can tear the deck into quarters.

Twenty-Six Drop Pop

I was sitting around with a bunch of old high school friends, talking about what we had all been up to recently. I mentioned some of the subjects that were going to be in this book. One of my friends said he had a real jewel for me. He picked up the whisky bottle that we had just emptied, turned it up side down and pounded the bottom of it with his palm to get every drop out of it. Then he handed the bottle to me and said to wave it around in the air until it was completely dry inside.

After getting tired of waving and being completely satisfied that the bottle was dry, I handed it back. He looked at the bottle and said that there were still twenty-six drops in it. He placed a napkin on the table and said: "Get ready to count them." He took out a lighter and ran the flame all around the outside of the bottle to heat it up.

Sure enough, the alcohol fumes turned to liquid and he poured out twenty-six drops. There was still another ten or fifteen drops left. He said they were for him, and drank them.

The Flies have it

Have a cup of coffee with a friend. Dip a piece of bread in your coffee and put it on the saucer. Ask your friend to do the same and challenge him that whoever attracts the most flies to his piece of bread wins. You could bet and win one hundred dollars a fly!

Secret: The secret: before you offer the bet, pour lots of sugar in your cup of coffee when your friend isn't looking.

The Edible Candle

You can make one from the fleshy part of an apple and a piece of walnut which will be used as a wick. (Walnut burns). Bon Appétit!

The Ice Candle

Mix in a test tube an equal part of water and ether, shake very well. Place the tube in a small container that holds an equal part of ice and salt. Once the candle is frozen, you can light it.

One Hundred Words Bet

Bet someone that you can quickly say one hundred words in a row without using the letters A, B, C, J, K, M, P, Q, Z.

Secret: Count from one to one hundred. None of these words contain the above letters. Or you could simply say "One hundred words, one hundred words" for an easy trick to play on pals.

The Big Hit

Here is a way to break a rock with your bare fist. Use a limestone rock and let it soak in water overnight. The limestone acts like a sponge, absorbing the water into its pores which will rot the stone. It is then placed on a flat surface. Now raise your hand closed into a fist, and hit it right in the middle with the side of the fist, not with your knuckles.

The stone instead of your hand should break into pieces.

Dry Coin

Pour enough water into a dinner plate to just cover a quarter and drop the quarter in. Challenge anyone to pick up the coin without getting their fingers wet.

Secret: It can be done. Cut a cork lengthwise so that it floats easily on its flat side. Then stick two lit wooden matches on top of the floating cork. Place a glass next to the quarter, on top of the burning matches and cork. A vacuum is created and the water will be sucked inside the glass. You can now pick up the quarter without getting your fingers wet.

Out of Reach

Here is a funny bar bet that you can't lose. Have someone stand against a wall with his heels touching it. Now place a ten dollar bill at his feet. Challenge him to pick up the bill without bending his knees or moving his feet. There is no way he'll be able to get it, so your bill is safe.

Secret: The reason he can't bend over is because the wall stops him from moving his back.

The Straw that Could Break the Camel's Back

Challenge a friend to lift a beer bottle with a straw without touching the bottle.

Secret: To do it, bend approximately one-third of the straw. Put the bent part of it inside the bottle. Wait until it unfolds, then lift the bottle slowly by holding the end of the straw that is sticking out.

Locked Knee

Ask someone to place his left side against a wall. The left foot, leg, and arm have to touch it. Now ask him to lift his right knee and to keep it up for a short while. He can't do it and he'll think his knee is locked.

Secret: Standing in this position against a wall stops you from shifting your weight; your left shoulder cannot turn away from the wall, therefore your right knee has lost its power.

Second Time Around

Have a lit candle on a table. Blow the flame out, then bring a lit match one inch above the candle wick; it will light again without being touched.

Secret: When the candle's flame goes out, the rising smoke catches the flame of the match.

Ping Pong Schnoz

Throw a ping pong ball in the air, catch it with your nose and keep it balanced while walking around the room. Impressed with yourself?

Secret: This one is an eye popper and it's soooo easy to do. Put a little dab of rubber cement on the tip of your nose so that when the ball hits, it sticks. Rubber cement is clear and won't be noticed unless you draw attention to it. Rubber cement is used on the skin in many illusions and special effects. I'm sure it's not good for you, but the only complaint I've heard is from those who have to take it off nightly because the constant peeling irritates the skin.

Paper Bridge

Place two glasses of equal height about five inches apart, and put a $1 bill on top of the two glasses. Now ask someone to position a third glass in the middle on top of the $1 bill without the glass dropping.

Secret: To make sure the $1 bill supports the third glass, crease it lengthwise like an accordion. It will then bear the weight of the glass.

Smoky Drink

Blow smoke from your mouth into a glass. Then pour the smoke into another glass. For the finale, you drink the smoke.

Secret: Since smoke is heavier than air, it will pour. This procedure needs to be done very slowly and gently. When pouring the smoke from one glass into the other make sure that the edges are touching. When "drinking" the smoke, blow air softly into the glass making the smoke disappear. To prove that you drank it, you can keep some smoke inside the mouth and blow it out later once the glass is empty. Cheers!

The Paper Boil

Make a cup from a tightly folded piece of paper and fill it half way with water. Bring a lit candle underneath it. The water will start boiling but the cup won't catch fire.

Glass and Science

Position a glass bottle in front of a lit candle. If you blow against the bottle, the candle flame goes out, even though you blow against a "wall."

Secret: The air currents from your breath are divided, but they join on the opposite side of the bottle to extinguish the flame.

Bend a Nail with Your Hands

To start, choose a light penny nail. After a few successful sessions, you'll be able to use stronger and bigger caliber nails. Place the nail on a piece of cloth, like a bandana or handkerchief, and wrap each end of it. The more wrapping you do, the safer it will be for your hands and the better grip you'll get on it.

This done, place the wrapped nail on your leg above a bent knee. By pushing each end down, bend it in the middle. Nails are easier to bend than most people think.

A Quarter is Too Heavy to Lift

You need a hard cover book, a regular wineglass, a bandana, and a quarter.

Place the book flat in the palm of one hand and hold it with the thumb. Put the wine glass on top of the book and spread the bandana on top to cover everything. Ask someone if he can lift the glass, which of course he can.

Now put a quarter inside the glass and spread the bandana to cover everything again. Under cover of the bandana, secretly move your index finger to hold the foot of the glass firmly with the thumb. When the person is asked to lift it again, he will have difficulty doing it, as though weight has been added to the glass.

Before showing the glass and book again, replace your index finger to its original position.

Spoon Boom

This is a bar bet I actually saw take place one time in Australia.

Sitting in a booth next to me were a tourist and an Aussie hustler. The hustler broke the ice with a story about how his father was driving down the road and hit a kangaroo. His father propped it up and put his jacket on the roo so he could get a picture taken with it. Right when he was preparing to pose, the kangaroo's eyes popped open and he hopped away into the bush wearing the jacket. He had only been stunned.

After a few beers, the hustler stuck the handle of a spoon between his teeth and tried rapping the spoon's end on the table. He took it out of his mouth and said: "It sure is difficult to hit something hard with the spoon between the teeth."

When it was time to order another beer, the hustler proposed that whoever can hit the other the hardest on the head with the spoon wins a beer. He told the tourist to put the spoon in his mouth. The hustler lowered his head and said: "OK, hit me as hard as you can." The tourist tried but it hurt his teeth. When it was the hustler's turn, and the tourist lowered his head, a friend of the hustler's came up from behind with a spoon in his hand and smacked the tourist sharply on the head. Since his head was down, he didn't know he was hit from behind, so he paid for the beer. It's amazing what people will do to get a free beer!

Dad's Favorite

There is no trick that I have seen more times than my dad's favorite prediction.

This trick is so simple that I'm worried that you might slap me after reading it. So before you raise a hand to take a swat at my face, try it.

Like my daddy used to say, "This will baffle'em." When guests visited, my father would point to an envelope with an ashtray on top of it and say: "Before you came over tonight I wrote a prediction on that envelope." He'd pick up salt and pepper shakers and say: "These two shakers look exactly alike, except for the initials on top. I want you to choose the "S" or the "P." After the selection, dad would go to the envelope and prove that he had predicted the right choice. At first, his friends would protest that he had a 50/50 chance. So my father told them that any time they came over he would have the envelope waiting. So from then on, every time they came over he would do it with different items like two cards "Pick the King Or the Jack," or "Pick either mustard or ketchup." It didn't matter, my father was always right.

Sorry dad, but I'm going to give the family secret away.

Secret: He would select two items ahead of time. Let's say quarters with different dates. He'd write one date on the envelope, and the other date on a piece of paper that he put inside the envelope. He'd set the envelope on the table with the date side facing down, and place the ashtray on top of it. It didn't matter which one they picked. If it was the date on the envelope, he would take the ashtray off and turn it over. If they picked the date on the paper, he would just reach in and pull it out.

With both bets covered, Pop's scam was better than 50/50!

Unusual Lighter

The next time someone asks you for a light, reach into your pocket and produce a flaming match from a matchbook.

Secret: To do this feat, have a prepared matchbook in your pocket. Bend a match forward from the top folder, then close it behind the bent match. When reaching for the matchbook, hold the back with your fingers, and press firmly the head of the bent match with your thumb on the striking surface until the match is lit.

Be careful, there have been many accidents to sensitive parts of the body due to the matches igniting in the pocket.

Smoke Produced From Sleeve

Anybody can blow smoke down a sleeve and make it come out of the other one.

Secret: Get a soft rubber tubing long enough to reach comfortably to each wrist under your long sleeve shirt. Make sure you can move your arms naturally. Tape each end of the tubing on your wrists, facing the palms of your hands. Now lift your right hand and blow the smoke through the tube. It will look like the smoke comes out of the other sleeve.

The Jerk

Put a plastic cup full of water on top of a napkin on a table. With a sharp jerk, the napkin can be pulled from under the cup without knocking it down.

Artificial Blizzard

Create an artificial blizzard with a wine glass and paper napkins.

Secret: Tear a paper napkin into small pieces. Take a good quality wine glass and rub it awhile with a silk scarf. Make sure all parts are rubbed. Now place the glass upside down and let the pieces of tissue paper drop down on the glass. They will stick to the glass. Once the electricity effect wears off, the scraps will jump off the glass.

One Through Ten

Here is a guessing trick that you will get right every time.

Tell someone that you can read his mind. Ask him to think of a number between one and ten and not to tell you what it is. Wait a few seconds and say: "OK, did you think of one?" They always say yes and you always win.

Gambling Scams and Card Sharps

Face-Up Poker

A hustler asks a mark if he'd bet a game of face-up draw poker.

He spreads a fifty-two card deck face up on the table and says: "I will reach in and pick out any five cards I want and then you reach in and pick out any five cards you want." The hustler says the dupe wins in the event of a tie, and that he'll let the dupe take his cards last. They agree the suits are all of the same value. Since the opponent gets to go last on both—deal and draw—it will seem like a sure bet for him to at least get a tie.

The best hand in poker is a royal flush, and to get a tie, all the dupe has to do is take a royal flush in another suit.

The hustler goes first and takes four tens plus a non-important card. The dupe is always surprised that he didn't take a royal flush. But after the tens are gone, he realizes that the best hands left are four of a kind higher than a ten or a straight flush, which are both better than the hustler's hand.

The four tens preclude the dupe from building a straight or a straight flush higher than a nine. The hustler then discards three of the tens and the odd card. The one ten will be used to build the highest straight flush left. The mark is totally caught off guard with that winning strategy.

The key for a hustler to get someone to take him up on this bet is the act. After watching a legitimate poker game and seeing someone lose, he acts drunk and says: "You're the worst player I've ever seen, you couldn't win even with the cards turned up, blah, blah, blah." He is careful to emphasize: "I will even give you all ties and let you go second so that you can see what I have ahead of time blah, blah." Going first insures the hustler a victory.

Marked Deck

An old con artist's trick is to mark cards so they can be identified by touch. *Bumping* is when you can feel bumps on the surface of the cards. Make a tiny dent with a pin. *Roughing* is when you rough up the edge of the cards with sandpaper.

By feeling the cards, both systems allow the dealer to always know what you have.

Monte Myth # 1

The Three-Card Monte is an old street con game. It works like this: the dealer holds a red queen and two black kings that he throws face down on a table or cardboard box. The rule is to guess which one is the queen. The victim puts his money down on the card he thinks is the winner, then the dealer turns it over to show which one it is. It appears to be a simple game to beat.

There is a general perception that street hustlers working the Three-Card Monte games always let you win the first time you play to get you hooked. This myth grew from seeing money changing hands with other betters. The other betters are in fact part of the scam. It is their job to make you feel comfortable enough to take out your money and try to beat the dealer.

When you first walk up to the game, you see a guy who is winning most of the time with great enthusiasm. He makes the game feel like it's a lot of fun and an easy way to make money. When he wins, you see how he did it. When he loses, you see where he went wrong. The dealer has a bag full of money stuffed in his pocket that he uses to keep his winnings and pay his losses. Since only one person bets at a time, the "other better" offers to let you play. If you accept, the dealer will hustle you out of twenty dollars on the first bet.

After a quick loss like this, you might take a step back to reassess your strategy. This allows our friend, the "other better," to start betting again. He loses three times in a row and out of anger throws the losing card. When the dealer turns his back to retrieve the card, the "other better" bends the corner of the winning card. When the dealer returns, the game starts again. This time the other player picks the bent card and wins every time.

After sustaining several losses, the dealer says: "That's enough, let someone else play," and he looks at you: "One last bet. Five hundred dollars limit. How much do you want to bet?" When you open your wallet, the "other better" excitedly snatches all your money and throws it on the bent card. The dealer turns the card over and you lose. He grabs the winnings, and puts it in his money bag that he stuffs back in his pocket. The dealer had secretly taken the bend out of the winning card.

When you start to argue to get your stolen money back, his partner, the "other better" screams "Police!" and takes off running. The dealer runs in the opposite direction. If you chase him he will throw his money bag. Once you get it, you'll find that it's a duplicate bag stuffed with newspaper and a rock. The rock adds enough weight to throw the bag far enough for the hustler to get away while you're chasing the bag.

Monte Myth # 2

Three-Card Monte is one of the easiest sleights to learn. You only have to lift your middle finger first when throwing the cards onto the table. The simplicity of this trick means many people know how to do it. They know exactly where the winning card is, but they never win. If they pick the right card, the dealer says: "Double or nothing?" That is the cue for his partner to slap the money on the table first. Since only one person is allowed to bet at a time, this negates the deal.

The Talking King

Ask a volunteer to place four cards facedown under four objects. Tell him you will use the help of the king of diamonds to guess each card. Slide the king face up under one card at a time and bring it to your ear where the king "whispers" the name of the card in question.

Secret: This trick is very simple to learn. First ask the volunteer to shuffle the deck. Once done, go through it to take the king of diamonds out. While doing that glance at the last four cards at the bottom of the deck and memorize them. Ask the volunteer to cut the deck, and to pick a half.

Whatever he chooses, make sure he ends up with the half that has the chosen cards. Then ask him to count the cards; this move will bring the four cards on top. Whatever the number of cards he comes up with, just say: "Yeah, that's about right." Ask him to put each of the four cards that are on top of the deck under four objects.

Now the rest is easy. Since you remember the cards, the king doesn't have to say anything.

If the Shoe Fits, Steal it

Show your audience the front and back of a playing card, let's say the ten of hearts. Place it on the floor face-up. Put your foot on top of it, fully covering it. Lift your foot again. Everyone is astonished to see the ace of diamonds instead.

Secret: Two cards are needed. The ace of diamonds is carefully and tightly held behind the ten of hearts as though both cards were one. Prior to the stunt, stick a piece of gum or beeswax on the sole of your shoe. Cover the card so it cannot be seen. When lifting the foot up, the ten of hearts will stick to the sole leaving the ace of diamonds on the floor.

Craps Props

Craps players pride themselves on their knowledge of the laws of probability, but they are not always prepared for a hustler's angle.

First, before getting into this, if you don't understand craps, then you should learn.

Second, never take a proposition bet.

Game # 1:

Any dice player knows betting on "hardways combinations" is a sucker's bet. So if a hustler approaches them with a proposal that if they will be the bank, he will only bet the "H.W. Combos." He says he will put two dollars on all H.W.'s, and every time they come up he gets casino odds. When hard four or ten (2-2 or 5-5) come up, he is to be paid off at 7 to 1 odds, which will give him $14.00 for his two dollar bet. When a hard six or eight come up, he is to get 9 to 1, which is eighteen dollars. Any time a seven, soft four, soft six, soft eight or soft ten is rolled, he will lose his two dollars and have to ante up again.

The key is that the hustler only loses two dollars. In a casino he'd have to bet eight dollars to cover all of the hard ways. The dupe always seems to over-look that important part and only hears the 7 to 1 and 9 to 1, which is the legitimate casino payoff. Even at two dollars the hustler can win a lot of money fast.

Game # 2:

This one is called "the bar six-eight game." The hustler tells the dupe that the six and eight will be void on the come out roll. Anytime the six and eight are rolled on the come out, it will be ignored and the dice will be rolled again. If the six and eight are barred, the dupe will want to bet against the dice, fading the shooter.

He will do this because he knows the six and eight are the easiest points for the shooter to make. But he forgets that in casino craps, the odds only favor the shooter on the come out, after that, they shift to the "don't" bet. But since the six and eight have been taken out it allows the hustler to roll over and increase the odds for instant wins from seven and eleven.

The experienced player will let the hustler throw all night thinking he has the best bet and that he's just going through a period of bad luck that will turn at any minute.

The Sure Bet

Forcing is a way to make a volunteer pick a par-
ticular object card while he thinks he had chosen
freely.

Every trickster should have several forces at their
disposal. Most require practice, but here is a simple
one to get you started: The performer takes out a
deck of normal cards and secretly peeks at the bottom one. He sets the cards on the table and says to
a volunteer: "There are fifty-two cards in a deck. I
want you to cut them to where you think there are
thirteen left on the bottom."

Then the performer picks up the bottom cut and
counts them one at a time, placing each card face
down on top of the cut that was left on the table,
until finished. It doesn't matter how many cards are
counted because the bottom card is now on top. The
performer tells him to look at the top card but not to
let him see it, and to shuffle it anywhere into the
deck. All the performer has to do is reach into the
pile and pull out the designated card.

Now you are ready for the greatest card scam ever
devised. It's better than Three-Card Monte. Let's say
the seven of clubs is on the bottom, it is brought to
the top, looked at and reshuffled into the deck by the
volunteer, and the force is complete.

Take the cards into your hands and start turning
them over one at a time, placing each card on top of
the previous one face up on the table. When you get to
the object card, in this case, the seven of clubs, don't

stop! Continue with four or five more cards on top. The volunteer will think you have made a mistake; that's when you look at the cards that are still in your hand and say: "I bet you twenty dollars that the next one I turn over is yours." They always bite because they have already seen their card on the table. After the twenty dollar agreement, reach into the stack of card on the table, find the seven of clubs and flip it over.

I have won thousands of dollars over the years doing this trick. I make the silly point of not betting, we have a laugh and I give them their money back.

Internet Gambling

Information about cards that you're not supposed to see can create an unbeatable advantage in poker. Millions of people around the world are being fleeced on internet gaming sites due to collusion. The sites all advertise that they have software that catches the patterns and bans the cheaters. The software detects the players that never go up against each other. Over time it does work if the team is only relaying information and fending for themselves. If the cheaters create a syndicate that shares all profits, then they have no fear of going against each other and cannot be caught. The penalty for being caught is getting kicked off the site. There are hundreds of sites with new ones being added daily. They do not share cheater information like Las Vegas casinos so it's not much of a penalty at all. Internet gambling has surpassed pornography. as the number one moneymaker on the world wide web. Expect this scam to grow.

THE NUMBERS GAME

All Numbers Lead to the Same One

This "number stunt" is one of the oldest and best. My father learned it from his father. No matter which number the volunteer chooses, the answer will always be 1089.

Secret: Here is how it works: Ask someone to write a 3-digit number and to reverse it. He has to subtract the small number from the large one. He then reverses the new number and adds the two together. The final total will always be 1089. Let's say he chose the number 851:

$$851 - 158 = 693 + 396 = 1089$$

If the first equation is 99, it has to be added to itself before continuing the calculation. For example, if the first number he chooses is 150:

$$150 - 51 = 99 + 99 = 198 + 891 = 1089$$

The 99 Presentation:

Tell him: "Write a 3 digit number, reverse it and subtract the small one from the large one. Now you have a 3-digit number, reverse it and add them together."

If the volunteer says that he only has a 2-digit number (the 2-digit number will always be 99), tell him: "OK, let's make it a bit harder. Whatever number you have, add it to itself. Then reverse the answer and add the two totals together." His final result will be 1089.

Knowing 1089 is always the answer can be used in many mind-reading feats.

My Favorite 1089 Force:

Get prepared ahead of time by memorizing the tenth word that is on page number eighty-nine of a chosen book.

When the person gets to the final total (he doesn't know that you already know the number is 1089), give him the book and ask him his number. Say: "Since the last two digits of your number are 89, go to page 89; and since the first two digits are 10, go to the tenth word."

Right when the volunteer is about to read the word, you say it aloud as if you were reading his mind.

Repeated Number

Tell someone to write the number twelve million three hundred forty five thousand six hundred seventy nine on a piece of paper: 12,345,679. This long number represents each digit except 8, so it won't be hard to memorize.

Ask him to circle the number that he thinks is his lucky one. Let's say 5. Mentally multiply the chosen number by 9 (5 X 9 = 45). You then ask the person to multiply your total by the long one. (In our example 45 X 12,345,679 = 555,555,555). The result will be a long series of the lucky number.

This works with each number, even 8.

100 to 999

Here is a simple "mind reading" game that you can do anywhere.

Hand a piece of paper to a volunteer and ask him to write a number between 100 and 999, without showing it to you. (Let's say he chooses 643). Proceed by asking him to reverse the number and to subtract the small one from the large one. (In our example 643 - 346 = 297).

Then ask the person the first digit of the final number. (In our example it is 2). After a few seconds of "concentration," you will guess correctly the final number.

Secret: The final results will always be:

99, 198, 297, 396, 495, 594, 693, 792, 891.

Once you know the first digit, it is very simple to guess the full number because if you add the first and last digits you get 9, which is the middle digit. The only exception is if the first digit given is 9, that means the number is 99.

Which Day is it?

Ask someone from the audience to give you a date. With some calculation you will be able to guess the exact day of the week the date falls on.

To start, you must learn a code that represents a number for the months, and a number for each day of the week.

Month	Value
June	0
September, December	1
April, July	2
January, October	3
May	4
August	5
February, March, November	6

Note: In Leap Years, January and February values are reduced by one.

Day	Value
Sunday	1
Monday	2
Tuesday	3
Wednesday	4

Thursday	5
Friday	6
Saturday	0

As an example, the date given to you is *May 5th, 1844*. Take the last two digits of the year (44) and add a quarter of it (11) which totals 55. Then add the value of the month (4 = May) which gives 59, next add the day of the month (5th) giving a new total of 64. Divide this new number by 7; the remainder will be 1. 1 represents Sunday.

May 5th 1844 was a Sunday.

If the last two digits of the year given by a spectator cannot be divided exactly by four, then take the closest lowest number divisible by four.

For example, let's take the year 1838. We use 36 as the closest lowest number that we can divide by 4. Then add a quarter of 36 (9) to 38 giving 47 to which the value of the month is added.

This example (*May 5th 1844*) applies for the nineteenth century 1801 to 1900.

When the given date happens to be in the twentieth century 1901 to 2000 subtract 2 from the last remainder; when the date is in the eighteenth century (1701 to 1800), add 2 to the last remainder.

Let's Recap:
Add the last 2 digits of the year to its quarter.
Add the code value of the month.
Add the date of the month.
Divide the total by 7.

The remaining number represents the day of the week. Subtract 2 from the last remainder if the date is in the 20th century. Or add 2 if the date is in the 18th century. *Other Examples:*

June 18, 1921: Add 21 to 5 (quarter), plus 0 (month), plus 18 (date) equals 44. Divide by 7; the remainder is 2. Subtract 2 for twentieth century = 0.

0 represents *Saturday.*

October 4, 1718: Add 18 to 4 (quarter), plus 3 (month), plus 4 (date) equals 29. Divide by 7, the remainder is 1; add 2 for eighteenth century. The number is 3 which represents *Tuesday.*

You can impress people by guessing the day of their wedding, birth, and so on.

Date Prediction

The medium holds two pocket size calendars. He hands one along with a pencil to an audience member, and keeps the other. The performer tells the volunteer to choose a month and to circle one date of the chosen month without showing it to him while the performer does the same.

The volunteer is then asked to say the date and month he chose. The medium shows him his calendar which has the same date circled.

Secret: The effect is done with a thumb tip writer. When the person is asked to circle his date, the performer pretends to do the same with a pencil. Once he hears the date, he circles it with the thumb tip. *(See Chapter 2).*

The same principle can be applied with many other feats of mentalism. The thumb tip writer provides an endless list of predictions and lots of fun.

Easy Mental Arithmetic

Ask an audience member for a three-digit number that you write twice on a black board. Let's say 391.

391   391

Then ask him for another three-digit number that you write under the first one that serves as a multiplier. Let's say 748.

391   391
x 748

And last *you* write a three-digit number under the second one that will also serve as a multiplier. Let's say 251.

391   391
x 748   x 251

Now you tell him that you can mentally do the two multiplications, add the two results together and come up with the total faster than he can with a calculator.

Secret: When he gives you the second three-digit number, (in our example 748), subtract each digit from 9 and write this new number as the second multiplier (in our example it would be 251):

$$391 \qquad\qquad 391$$
$$\times\,748 \qquad\qquad \times\,251$$

While the volunteer is busy multiplying and adding, you subtract 1 from the first three-digit number, and write down the result. (In our example it will be 391 - 1 = 390).

Then subtract each digit of the last result from 9. (In our example subtract the digit of 390 from 9 which gives 609).

You now write this last result (609) to the right of the last number (390) and you get the final total.

In our example the final total is 390,609.

This can be done with any three-digit numbers if this formula is applied.

CARNIVAL GAMES

Strung Out

This is a carnival game where customers have a chance to win great prizes. The operator holds a collar with strings coming from it and attached to prizes. The other side of the collar has the strings attached to tabs. When the customer pulls a tab, the appropriate string draws the prize connected to it.

The prizes are the usual junk, like balls, mirrors, cheap plush toys, along with some higher quality ones like TV's, walkmen, radios, etc. To show you can win any of these, the vendor pulls all the strings at the same time, so all the prizes move. But every time a customer pulls a tab, he only gets a cheap prize.

Secret: What happens is the strings are tricked. They are all attached to the collar, but only the ones

119

attached to cheap prizes have tabs. Therefore nobody can win the expensive items.

Getting Nailed

Here is another carnival game that seems totally honest.

The object of this nail-hammering game is to hammer a nail into a piece of wood with just one blow. The operator takes a nail from his carpenter's apron and does the feat easily. He repeats the process a few times. He then lures victims to do the same. For some reason, they can never do it as successfully.

Secret: The secret lies in the type of nails used. The operator uses a hard nail which he takes from his apron. As for the victims, he gives them soft ones that are taken from a secret pocket in his apron.

Basket Case

The vendor lures people up with a carny pitch. For just one dollar, they can toss 3 balls into a basket. If the three stay inside the basket, they can win a portable TV; with two inside, lesser quality prizes; with one or none they lose. To show how easy it is, the vendor tosses 3 balls that stay inside the basket. But once the customer tries, the balls don't seem to stay inside.

Secret: The baskets have reinforced wood bottoms that make the balls bounce out. Also, the baskets are tilted at an angle that disadvantage the thrower. Ninety percent of the time the balls will hit the upper-half of the basket bottom and bounce out.

Finally, the vendor is at a better advantage since he's behind the counter where the angle is different. The balls will bounce from side to side and settle to the bottom.

The Bottle Toss

This game can also be seen at carnivals and state fairs. The object is not only to knock the wooden bottles down, but to throw them off their pedestals with one hit.

They are positioned in a form of a pyramid: 3 at the bottom, 2 above, and one at the very top. A lead-weighted bottle can be easily knocked over, but rarely off the pedestal. So why can the operator always demonstrate it as though it were easy?

Secret: When the victim does it, the lead-weighted bottles are positioned on the bottom row, which takes more hits to throw them off. But when the operator demonstrates it the three lead-weighted bottles are positioned on the two top rows of the pyramid, making it easy to knock them off with one hit.

Age Guessing

This is a game that's still seen at carnivals or fairgrounds where people pay two dollars to have their age guessed. If the guesser is wrong, the customer gets a prize.

The performer tells the audience that he can guess someone's age within two years. This range gives him the advantage. Let's say the performer guesses the customer to be 29 years old, he wins if that person is between 27 and 31.

Here are clues he looks for:

Friends: Knowing the type of people the customer came with could indicate the age range. For example, a group of teenage girls could give up the age of their friend who's trying to look older.

Hair Color: Some people's hair becomes gray prematurely but if gray appears on the mustache or beard, the person is older.

Face: The guesser brings the customer in the light, so he can look at the face better. He tries to make the person smile to see if age wrinkles show.

Hands: The performer looks for age spots, especially in the case of an older woman who has had cosmetic surgery and looks younger than her hands.

The Cheater:

Sometimes the performer will cheat. He writes two numbers on a pad and asks the person their age. He then shows him the right number (or the closest to the truth) while hiding the other one with his thumb. With the two year range allowed, he has a huge advantage.

Let's say he writes 26 and 31. It allows him to win every time if the customer is between the age of 24 and 33.

Another Way to Guess the Age:

The guesser asks a volunteer to write his age on a piece of paper without showing it. He tells him to add 752 to his age, since there are 7 days in a week and 52 weeks in a year. Then he tells him to add 12 to the result since there are twelve months in a year.

He finishes by asking the volunteer the last digit of the final total. The guesser immediately tells the exact age.

Secret: This method works with a mix of simple calculation and observation.

The guesser subtracts 4 from the digit given by the volunteer (if the digit is smaller than 4, he adds 10 to it before subtracting 4). Whatever the final number the guesser gets, it will be the last digit of the volunteer's age.

For example: If the last digit given is 6; subtract 4 from it which gives 2. If the volunteer looks like he's in his twenties, his age is 22.

The Weight Guess

Once again the advantage goes to the performer who tells the audience that he can guess their weight within three pounds. The key is a one week concentrated effort to learn how your friends weights correspond to their frames.

He first compares the customer's frame with someone he knows. He looks at the wrists and arms to see if the person has small or big bones. He checks if the customer is wearing baggy or tight fitting clothes; he looks for bulges and big muscles.

And last he knows that women who don't mind having their weight guessed in public are usually thin.

Baby Show

Here is another attraction on the midway.

To get people in, the "Baby Show" has several banners and a tape loop. "See the world's most bizarre babies," "The children of forgotten fathers," "See the two-headed baby, the frog baby, and Cyclops," "Come see why they did not ask to be born."

As a psychological touch, a baby stroller is parked in front of the tent implying the children were alive.

These deformed babies are actually made out of rubber and called "pickled punks" or "bouncers." They are immersed in a blue liquid inside medical jars.

Hoop and Block Game

Seen at carnival and state fairs.

The object is to throw a hoop around a metal stick. This game is almost impossible to win because the hoop is tossed by the customers from the wrong angle.

The operator always wins because he's inside the counter and much closer to the stick enabling him to practically drop the hoop during his demonstration. The rest is just toss acting.

Go Fishing

This is a typical fishpond game found at carnivals, state fairs, and amusement parks where about 100 wooden fish float down a small stream past the counter. The customer pays for a fish that has a hidden number on its underbelly. Each number corresponds to a winning prize; some of them higher quality than others. As usual, everyone's a winner. But in this classic example, what looks right to you is really upside down.

Let's say your winning number is 66 and it corresponds to a radio, the vendor will hold the fish the other way and call it 99 for an ashtray. The other upside numbers used are: 9 for 6; 16 for 91; 18 for 81;89 for 68; 98 for 86.

The Mark

It was while working at the fairground as a kid that I learned the origin of the term "easy mark." There would always be some drunks tossing out wads of money hoping to win at the games, but they'd always lose. The operator would pat the guy on his shoulder and wish him better luck next time around. Unbeknownst to him, the comforting hand had chalk on it, clearly marking him as a sucker to the other vendors.

The Geek Act

The geek act can at times become a rowdy affair due to disappointed customers. The presentation makes them feel like they are going to see a wild man from Borneo eating live chickens. Instead there is a guy, a chicken, and a dirty half-full porta-potty in a cage. The cage is there to protect the performer from the audience, instead of the other way around.

As soon as everyone is in the tent, he grabs the chicken, bites its neck lightly, to reopen a small cut, and smears blood and feathers on his face. But before the customers can lynch him for letting them down, he grabs the porta-potty and splashes it on everyone until they exit the tent in a mad rush.

The liquid was only dirty colored water, but it works.

STREET SCAMS

Beware of this One!

A hustler finds a dupe and shows him some card sleights. He informs him that there is a wealthy guy who loves to play cards. The scammer says: "I can cheat this guy out of a lot of money, but I need someone to work with me." The dupe asks what he can do to help. The hustler says: "Every time I shuffle and deal, you will win, so bet everything you have when I shuffle. Also, I lost my ass at the horses last week, so you'll need $2,000, it will look like we have money. Remember, only bet high when I do the dealing. After we take this guy to the cleaners, we'll split the money later. It can be as much as $10,000 a piece for a night's work. Not bad, eh?"

The dupe gets all excited and withdraws $2,000 and shows up at the poker game. What he doesn't know is the hustler and "the wealthy guy" are working together. The game goes just like the hustler promises; every time he shuffles, the dupe wins because the "wealthy guy" folds. After hours of playing, the dupe is winning the antes but he is only up $50. $50 isn't much if you are expecting to split $20,000.

This is when the hustlers take advantage. The "wealthy guy" can also manipulate cards. When it's his turn to deal, he stacks the deck giving the dupe 4 queens and an ace, while giving himself 4 kings. With 4 queens in his hand the dupe gets excited and raises the bets until reaching his $2000. They turn over their hands and the "wealthy guy" collects the money and leaves hastily. His partner, the con man who started the whole thing, yells in anger at the dupe: "I told you to bet only when I'm dealing the cards. You blew it." The dupe has just lost $2000 but feels lousy for letting his partner down.

Afterwards the hustler and "the wealthy guy" meet and cut up the money.

Chalk One Up

This scam is often seen in European cities where "artists" make exact replicas of classical paintings with colored chalk. They tape paper to the sidewalk to draw on, all day long people show their support by dropping tips or buying the finished replica.

Secret: What "chalk artists" really do is buy color copy photos of classical paintings and chalk over a bunch of them beforehand. On the street they act like they're chalking while collecting tips until someone buys one. Then they tape another one down and start all over again.

Short Change

The hustler goes up to the cashier and hands her a 10 dollar bill for a pack of gum. Right when she gets the change out of the register, he reaches into his pocket and says: "I have the right change for the gum." He puts the change on the counter and says: "Keep the ten I gave you and my change that you have in your hand and give me back a twenty."

If there is a line behind the hustler, or if the cashier is distracted at all, the hustler usually walks out with ten dollars profit.

The Oopsy

This is a short change technique used by crooked cashiers in a wide variety of businesses. It works well especially in a bar. A man pays for his drink with a 10 or 20 dollar bill. The crooked bartender gives him the change with some coins and one dollar bills. He counts them in front of the customer, straightening the bills by tapping them on the bar, then he places them in a neat pile in front him.

Now, the customer either puts the money in his pocket right away, since he's seen it counted, and is sure the amount is accurate, or leaves it on the bar for future drinks.

What actually happens is the customer is being robbed right before his eyes without knowing it.

Secret: While tapping the money on the bar to straighten the bills the bartender secretly drops one on his side of the bar, which he picks up later. If the drinker notices, the bartender says "oops," and returns the bill apologizing as if it were an accident.

A Dog Called Unlucky

A stranger shows up at a bar with a nice looking dog. He informs the bartender that the dog is a rare breed. He says he is in town for an important meeting and offers the bartender twenty dollars to watch his dog for two hours. Before leaving, the stranger reminds the bartender how valuable the dog is and to take good care of it.

A little later, another stranger comes in and shows great interest in the dog, and asks the bartender if he can buy it. The bartender refuses, telling him that the dog is not for sale. The stranger keeps insisting and offers 600 dollars. He tells him that he will come back in two hours to see if a deal can be worked out.

After the stranger leaves, the dog's owner comes back with a story about a horrible business meeting and now he's broke. The bartender, recalling the 600 dollar offer, sees a way to make a profit and offers money for the dog. The stranger refuses, saying it is too valuable and can't accept the offer. But the bartender insists anyway, until the dog owner agrees to sell the dog for 300 dollars. The dog owner takes the money and meets up with his partner, "the stranger," a few blocks away to split the money. The bartender ends up with a 300 dollar mutt.

So if a bartender does "The Oopsy" to you, get him back with "A Dog Called Unlucky"!

The Ring Sting

The Ring Sting requires two hustlers, we will call them Fred and Bill.

Bill drives up to a gas station, dressed in his Sunday best. After paying for two dollars worth of gas and using the restroom, he comes out whelping about how somewhere on the lot he lost his wife's diamond ring that he was going to get repaired. He frantically gets the gas station attendant to help him look all over the place for it. After a thorough and frustrating search, he leaves his phone number along with an offer of a $400 reward for its return.

Fifteen minutes later Fred walks up, dressed like a bum, and asks to use the restroom. He then walks up to the gas station attendant with a diamond ring in his hand and says: "Look what I found by the can, I bet it's worth 200 dollars. Do you want to buy it?"

In most cases the attendant remembers the 400 dollar reward and heads straight to the cash register to get the 50% investment.

By the time he figures out that the ring is a six dollar Woolworth special and the phone number is to a pay phone down the street, they are long gone.

Alerts

People tend to drive more slowly in alleys. Hustlers know this and often sneak out of the bushes while you're driving by to smack your car loudly and fall to the ground screaming in agony. When you stop to help they demand cash angrily for their injury.

It's their alley and their neighborhood. It's safer just to pay the fifty dollars and leave, than to get into a fight.

Ladies, when you park your car and go in to exercise or shop, someone may be watching. He will pop the hood and disconnect a wire. When you come out and can't start the car, he will come up and offer some help. After tinkering around under the hood he will say: "This usually costs about a hundred and fifty dollars to fix, but let me get my screwdriver and see what I can do."

After acting like a lot of work is being done he will tell you to try and start the engine. This will put you behind the wheel and unable to see how easy it is to pop the connector back on. When the car starts he will try to get twenty dollars for his time or a date or both.

Another unscrupulous way that the slime meet girls is by running *secretarial help wanted ads* with very high pay and stating "must be able to travel." It's the travel part that lets them know you are probably single.

Three Penny Smack

This scam requires 2 people working together. One goes into a bar and strikes up a conversation with somebody. The other acts like a drunk and stays outside. The drunk walks in later and becomes part of the conversation without acting like any of them know each other.

The drunk acts surly. He offers to flip pennies for a drink. The two "evens" have to buy the "odd" a drink. While the drunk isn't looking, the hustler tells the victim: "This guy is so drunk, he doesn't know what's going on. You flip first, the drunk second and I'll flip third. It doesn't matter what I flip because he's too drunk to see. So I'll call whatever is needed for one of us to win. Let's have some fun with this guy and get some free drinks."

Of course the fake drunk is conveniently out of ear shot while his partner is telling the victim how to win. The drunk loses along with the victim, so they pitch into buying the hustler his drink.

While the drunk goes into the bathroom as planned, the hustler says to the victim: "See how easy it was?" and gives him his money back. When the drunk returns, he pulls out a wad of cash and challenges them to a bet. The hustler whispers to the victim that they will split the winnings. Sure enough, the hustler is the "odd" man. The drunk and the victim pay up. The hustler winks at the victim and motions for them to go outside.

Just when they start to split the money, the drunk walks out and says: "Hey you two are con men. You cheated me out of my money. I'm going to call the police." The hustler says: "No, no, don't call the cops, we just met at the same time you walked up." The drunk: "Well then, you walk on out of here, and I will stay with your friend for a few minutes to make sure." The hustler agrees and whispers to the victim that he will be back in thirty minutes to split the money with him.

The drunk walking out at the perfect time is the "blow off." The "blow off" is used to give the guy with the money the time to get away. The story ends when the fake drunk meets up with the hustler to split the victim's money.

As with most cons, the mark thought he saw an opportunity for easy cash but instead he got cheated. There is some truth in the old saying: "You can't cheat an honest man."

Bon Appétit!

Ever been really hungry for steak and lobster, but didn't think you could afford it? Some people never worry about money. They don't dine and dash unless there's an open window in the bathroom. They are far more clever and have a plan.

For example: The hustler sits down, eats dinner and gets the check. When no one is looking, he puts the check in his pocket, stands up and acts like he sees something on the floor. He bends over and "finds" a ring under his table. He goes to the people sitting closest and says: "I just found this ring under my table. I'm going to give it to the manager in case someone comes back to claim it. I'm going to point where I found it. When you see me pointing to you, just wave so he knows the area where the ring was found."

The hustler secretly puts the ring back into his pocket and walks up to the host. He talks for a minute about the weather or something, and says: "Those nice people are picking up my check." When he points to the people who were sitting by him, they wave back. Then the con artist walks out with a free dinner in his stomach.

This next *"belly buster"* takes two people. The first person walks in to a Denny's, sits at the counter and orders a steak dinner. A few minutes later his friend walks in and sits next to him and orders a cup of coffee. They act like they don't know each other. When no one is looking, they switch checks. The person who ate the steak dinner takes the coffee check to the cashier, pays for it and walks out. After he has had enough time to get away, the coffee drinker turns his steak dinner check over and complains that all he had was coffee. He refuses to pay for a steak dinner he did not eat. The two hustlers meet up later and go to another restaurant and reverse the roles so they can both have a free meal.

It's in the Mail

To some these methods are too troublesome. They prefer going to the post office to pick up their free goods instead. First, they write down the customer service addresses of all the products they use. Then they send complaint letters to each of them. It's usually standard practice for the companies to settle the grievance by sending a free coupon to replace the faulty product.

Homeless and Rich

It's painfully obvious that most panhandlers are destitute and living the existence of our nightmares: derelicts, addicts, or victims of horrible luck barely scraping by. Their only moments of peace are their nightly naps in the gutter. These poor souls should be helped as much as possible. Unfortunately, a lot of well intended donations get into the wrong hands.

A good panhandler can make six figures. One sure way is to have a *female partner*. He then approaches people with a hard luck story connected with his new bride who is now two months pregnant.

Another old trick they use is to rub *globs of vaseline* in their eye lashes and act blind. The New York police call them "blinkies."

Keep the Receipt

The hustler goes to a dry cleaning establishment. When the cleaner turns his head, he reaches over the counter and steals his receipt book. Once outside he writes, "$19.95 Stain Removal Sweater," on a receipt.

He then goes to a restaurant with a story about his wife who had been in a week ago. She got mustard on her new sweater, and the waitress told her to get it cleaned and bring back the receipt. He acts embarrassed because his wife is making him do this.

Since the receipt is under twenty dollars, they usually give him the money. Hustlers have been known to scam as many as five restaurants an hour.

The Yard Stick to Riches

Ever go to a gas station or store with a yard stick and swipe it under the vending machines? It's one of those socially embarrassing types of treasure hunt, but very rewarding. You usually can knock several quarters your way.

Airport Taxi Scam

You're waiting for your luggage and a clean cut guy comes up asking if any one needs a taxi. If you say yes, he'll ask where you're going and about how much luggage you have. He will give you a quote for a few dollars less than normal fare and start to help you with the luggage.

Once outside he'll ask for the money. After collecting he'll hail a taxi and talk to the driver for a few seconds telling him your needs. Then he opens the door for you to get in, shuts it, and starts putting the luggage in the trunk. When finished he shuts the trunk and waves good-bye, keeping one of your bags and all of the taxi fare. By the time you and the taxi driver figure it out, he's already in a bar wearing your clothes and spending your money.

If you made the mistake of leaving your I.D in the bag, well, there are whole books written about what happens when the wrong person gets your I.D.

I Know I can Trust You, Right?

Two men become partners and open a store together. They alternate shifts; one works the cash register while the other sleeps. One day this old lady
walks in and picks up a ten dollar item, and leaves
a twenty dollar bill on the counter. She turns around
and starts walking out of the store. Right when she
gets to the door, the cashier is faced with an ethical
question. Should I tell my partner?

Studies have proven that for whatever reason, 70%
of business partnerships don't work.

Shoe Gazer

Here's a good one. Challenge anybody that you
can tell their future by reading the bottom of their
shoe. You take the shoe, look at it and say: "I see
that you will be taking a short trip very soon." You
then toss the shoe, making the person go retrieve it.

May I Use the Phone?

A person comes to your home or office with a
story about his car that broke down. He asks to use
your phone for help. A month later you get a 1-900
phone bill. The hustler uses as many people's phones
for as long as possible because he gets a percentage.

The Perfect Time Waster

No trick in the history of man has ever been more
senseless, useless, or ridiculous! This trick is done only
by those who are bored out of their minds. It can only

be mildly interesting to those locked in a room with each other for a couple of years. Like a jail.

Still interested? Okay then, you've just heard the guard say, "Lights out in five minutes." You and your cellmate, let's call him Louis, finish off the last of your contraband Scotch Whiskey, and light a cigarette. You start drifting off into a dreamlike state, thinking about tomorrow, roll call, and hope the soap won't slip from your hands. But instead of kissing Louis on the lips and saying good night, you come up with an experiment.

You fill the Whiskey bottle full of smoke by blowing it slowly in with a straw. You then ask Louis how long he thinks it would take for all the smoke to leave the bottle. Whatever he says, it will be wrong, because all you have to do is drop a lit match into the bottle. It will come in contact with the Whiskey residual and create a flash or mini explosion forcing the smoke out instantly.

CONSUMER SCAMS

Tooth Ache

Beware of dentists. They are quickly becoming the used car salesmen for the twenty-first century. Always get a second opinion.

Telemarketing

Hustlers acting like Gulf War vets call businesses to ask for help with their charity. Most businesses are barraged with calls like these and usually have a secretary screen them.

To get around the screen the hustler will say: "This is Mr. Howard I.R.S.; put the owner on the phone please."

When the owner gets on the phone, the hustler starts his presentation with a slight name change making it seem like the secretary made a mistake. "Hello Sir, this is Howard Iris with a Gulf War charity." He then will drop the phone, rattle it around a little and say: "I'm sorry, the phone cord got stuck in the spokes of my wheelchair."

Another telemarketing scam uses television shows that periodically run consumer alert segments. The shows always seem to concentrate on bottled water, high octane gas, and aspirin scams.

Most people think that their tap water is more impure than *bottled water*. This is untrue except for rare cases.

High octane gas is a flat out rip-off. Always buy the so-called low-grade petro and you won't notice the difference.

Aspirin is aspirin. I'm not trying to be redundant, but so many people have a mental picture of scientists tinkering with aspirin to improve it. There is no difference between aspirin brands; you pay extra for the names so their marketing and packaging costs are covered.

Coin Collectors

There is a new breed of underground coin collectors who are getting rich from everything that is coin operated. Their life's work is to constantly keep abreast of coin and token sizes from all over the world. They take advantage of conversions.

For example, if a coin worth 1/2 cent in Africa happens to be the same size as a U.S. quarter, then they sweep the U.S buying and reselling vending machine items. This is also being done in other countries. The English Pound which is worth $1.20 is vulnerable because its size is easy to get in cheaper currencies.

Coin and token sizes change almost daily somewhere in the world creating a bonanza for these guys.

Money from Your Nose

The fresh scent of popcorn you smell popping in the microwave is fake.

The fresh scent of bread wafting onto the street in front of a bagel or bakery shop is also usually fake.

Many products are now exploiting scent as a subliminal sales tool. They hire manufacturers who enhance the smells of their products. When your nose comes in contact with the scent, you salivate and are more likely to make the purchase.

Urine Test

Here is a story of a guy I met at the fairground when I was a kid. His name was Eb and he was doing a geek act amongst other things; he was also a drug addict. I was told a story about an unconventional way to beat a urine test.

Eb was in so much trouble that for awhile he had
to do urine tests twice a week. He'd get in fights
with people who sold him dirty urine, which caused
him to flunk the tests. It was a big laugh on the midway. Everyone was making fun of him.

One carny told him that the only way he could
find clean urine was to bet his little nephew a
quarter that he couldn't pee in a jar. The carnies
started to act like they cared, and told him they
were going to help him find clean urine. So every
time people walked by, they would point them out
and say: "That person looks clean, go ask him for
some." Or: "Stay away from that person, she looks
dirty."

After awhile, as people walked by, the carnies
could be heard saying to each other under their
breath: "Clean, clean, dirty, clean, dirty, dirty." They
would argue their assessments like: "That old lady is
dirty, look, she has a limp, she's on some kind of a
prescription." Or: "That guy's naively dirty, his urine
will be clean in a couple of weeks. He's just experimenting right now."

Somehow Eb came up with clean urine. So he
bought one of those small Elmer's glue bottles with
the twist cap. He emptied it out, sterilized it and
painted it flesh-colored. Then he filled it with the clean
urine, and put it in his Jockey shorts against his body
to keep it warm. At the test he reached into his
underwear with the hand closest to the monitor (the
person who's supposed to be watching to make sure

the urine isn't switched). He palmed the Elmer's bottle in his hand and squeezed it into the cup.

DRUG SCAMS

A dope fiend would kick the gold fillings out of his mother's mouth to get money for drugs. If they can be that ruthless, imagine what they do to each other. There is no honor amongst thieves in the narcotic community.

Cocaine rip-offs take an *Esquire* magazine cover for its rigid stock and make the kind of folds that are used to seal the drug. They put flour in it and barely crease the middle of the bundle. When customers open it, the fold pops up and sends the flour flying in all directions. The customers can only blame themselves and have to pay for their accident.

Some hustlers make volume purchases of white powdered *caffeine and procaine* mixtures from companies listed in the back of High Times magazine. Many of these companies sell or can get chemicals that they do not advertise. The white cocaine rip-off powder is put in a coffee filter and placed on top of a running coffee maker. The steam moistens it just enough for it to dry into rock form, making it look much more real and valuable.

Growers of marijuana have found a way to use most of the plant. In the old days only a quarter of the marijuana plant was considered to be of high enough quality to sell. Most of the plant was thrown out. Now they sell the no-quality parts to hustlers.

These *marijuana rip-offs* take an empty spray bottle
with 1/4 of pine scent and 3/4 of coca-cola. After
spraying the marijuana with the coke-pine mixture,
they compact it tightly into shoe boxes until it dries.
When dry, they peel the box away and break up the
marijuana into what looks and smells like expensive
high quality buds.

If the quality of the marijuana is so bad that all
the doctoring in the world can't make it look like
"greenbud," they will soak it in peroxide until it turns
brown and add some hemp seeds they take out of
bird feed. It is then back to coca-cola, pine scent and
shoe box compression. This time when they break it
up, it looks like "Mexican bud."

Opium poppies grow all over the world in gardens,
and it's usually legal as long as you don't use them
to get high. The seeds are easy to get and they make
beautiful plants. Most people don't realize that the
summer pods are full of narcotic. Junkies know exactly what these plants look like, and steal them from
gardens or grow them themselves.

"GET OUT OF JAIL FREE" CARDS

The Injury

Nothing upsets law enforcement officers more than a wise guy who beats the system. Here are a couple of the lesser known scams.

Many drunks have gotten out of DWI's by faking an injury. When a policeman pulls them over and asks them to get out of the car, they bump their head on the inner roof of the car, close their eyes and fall over. They don't open their eyes until they're sober.

This tactic usually results in a sixty dollar ambulance ride. In most states a blood test is not taken unless the person is seriously injured.

Shockabi

Many drunks who get in accidents that don't result injury go to a bar to order three or four drinks that they dump out when no one is looking. After establishing their alibi, they call the police to report the accident. They tell a story about how they went into shock during the accident and had stumbled to a bar for a few drinks to calm the nerves. The police can't prove if they had gotten drunk before or after the accident.

Some people don't like talking to the police at all when they're drunk, so they wait until the next day and report their car stolen.

Excuse Me

A defense that has worked in many DWI cases is to say that you burped when you took the breathalyzer. Burping forces more alcohol into the breathalyzer making the record inaccurate. The skewed logic is if you're drunk anyway, you might as well knock the needle off.

Speed

There are some people who break the speed limit on purpose. They are not drunk, it's a sport to them and they rarely get a ticket.

When pulled over, they get out of their car and start looking around at the tires. When the policeman walks up, the hustler talks first and says: "Officer, I'm having problems with my breaks, would you follow me to a gas station?"

The policeman will either consider it his civic duty, or suggest that it's too dangerous and the car should be towed. Either way he won't give him a ticket and doesn't have time to wait with him for the tow truck.

VANISH

People who think they are very clever usually end up running away from something, and are in need of a new life.

Locating a New Identification: The best way is to choose an identity of a person who died very young. Some hustlers use the obituary section in old newspapers found at libraries. Once they find someone about their age and sex, they take down all the pertinent information.

Some info like parents names and mother's maiden name can also be found at the U.S.. Census Bureau, hospital records, or church baptismal records.

Birth Certificate: They file for a duplicate birth certificate to replace the one they have "lost." It never arouses suspicion because the lack of an original birth certificate is so common in this country. The U.S. Passport office provides information on how to request a certified copy for a fee. After getting the birth certificate, everything opens up to them, all under a new name.

Driver's License: Once they get the birth certificate, they go to the Department of Motor Vehicles and get a driver's license.

Passport: They easily obtain it once they have proper identification and a birth certificate.

Social Security Number: They never use the same social security number twice. Every time they are asked they make up a new one.

Where They Hide: They go to big cities. It's easier for them to stay lost there than settling in a small town with nosy neighbors. There are also more job opportunities, public transportation, etc.

Finding Work: To build references, they do low-paying or part-time jobs. If they have valuable skills, they free-lance their services until they build up enough references to get a decent full-time job. They avoid jobs that are similar to previous employment. They usually seek temporary agencies and temporary work because they eventually lead to a full-time job. They avoid all jobs that put them in the public eye, like entertainment, bartending, hotel desks, etc.

Job Reference: Usually no more than two or three job references are required to get work. The hustlers get two or three mailbox addresses with fake company names. They write their own letters of reference on letterheads printed with the fake names.

If they are asked for a phone number, they give a friend's number who poses as a former employer, or they use a secretarial service that always says the person is not available, and will take a message. If in need of educational credentials, they either buy the degrees by mail order or they go through the educational process to get a new set of degrees and diplomas.

Disguise: To become unrecognizable, they try to become the opposite of what they were. They usually change their hair and the type of clothing; gain or loose weight; wear or remove eyeglasses; take on smoking or quit; grow or shave a beard. They hide scars, marks and tattoos with makeup or hair. Sometimes they change the way they walk by placing objects inside one shoe.

In extreme cases they get cosmetic surgery to change their features. They adjust their speech or change their accent or dialect to fit in with their new surroundings.

In all cases they are chameleons who avoid attracting any attention to themselves. The successful ones never have their photos taken and are careful with paper trails (always use mail boxes for all correspondence).

Also, they totally separate themselves from their original existence. And most of all, they never reveal their secret to anyone because that makes them vulnerable to apprehension or blackmail.

One, Two, Three,
on Billy Hiding Behind that Door

Ever met someone you wished you knew more about but didn't want to get a private investigator involved?

The full name, last known address, birthdate, and social security number can easily and legally be obtained. There are many cross-reference systems available at the library that have the names and addresses listed. A simple form letter and a small fee to the Register of Voters, the county courthouse, and property tax division, will provide a data search allowing you complete access to divorce decrees, garnishments, child support, mortgage holders, and just about anything else. These records should satisfy your initial goal, but hey, why stop here?

From the Motor Vehicle Dept. you can get moving violations, accident records, height, weight, sex, and color of eyes and hair. The last bit of information you will need to finish this phase is a T.R.W. report. T.R.W. is a national credit information company. For a small fee you can access their data base system. It is so complete that often times they know more about people than the people know about themselves.

You should now have a pretty good official profile of this person. Your next step is to make inventive phone calls to the numbers that have crossed your path. Talk to ex-fellow employees, school mates and family members. Soon you will have enough information to write a book about this person. Access to information in other countries is a little different but the same strategic formula works.

Pick Pocket Psychology

At some carnivals and state fairs thieves stand by a "Beware of Pickpockets" sign. They know that guys will read it and instinctively feel for their wallet. This alerts them to the placement of the money. They will then bump the victim once to make him grab his pocket. The wallet will still be there, and the guy will feel embarrassed about how paranoid he just acted. Now he's psychologically set up for the real heist.

Body Language

We are not born with trust. Trust has to be earned.

The Human Lie Detector:

We all wonder at times if people are telling the truth. Next time you're in doubt, look for these body language signs: nervous restlessness, wringing and clinching of hands, contradiction of composure, looking calm with a nervous voice or vice-versa, shifting of the eyes, sincerity of laughter.

The Eyes have it:

Gamblers use the information written above all the time in Poker. They are called "tells."

One of the most commonly used "tells" is the dilation of the pupils. If they get big, it usually means the player is excited because he holds a good hand. If the gambler raises his bet and his pupils are small, that means he's probably bluffing.

The understanding of the pupil dilation can also be used every day. Although it varies from person to person, you can use it as a measuring instrument to gauge how people around you feel. Next time you're not sure about someone being attracted to you, check the size of his/her pupils. It might be a good indicator. It can also work for salespeople, they can check your pupils to see if you're excited about a product.

First Impression

Bad first impressions can be rooted in truth and are hard to overcome. Appearance, posture, facial expression, and dress are important, so the next time someone says, "you can't tell a book by its cover," ignore it.

Recent studies have proven that first impressions are accurate 67% of the time. It is considered to be a trustworthy sixth sense. It can increase to almost 100% accuracy once we hear the person talk.

So remember what they say, "you only get one first impression."

The Handshake

People underestimate how much we can learn from a simple handshake. Here are some interpretations of my favorite squeezes:

#1: The *dead handshake* is the most confusing of all. Often times it is taken as a sign of shyness, but that is not always the case. The person in fact may not be feeling well, doesn't like you, is depressed, or has a general lack of interest in your acquaintanceship.

When faced with this shake, revert back to other body language signals to make an assessment. The other handshakes are much more reliable and informative.

#2: If the handshake is *quick and abrupt*, the person is asking for a formal relationship.

#3: A person who *grips your hand as firmly as you grip his/hers*, says he/she wants to cooperate.

#4: The *enthusiastic firm handshake* says: "I'm confident that I am the boss around here."

If during any of these handshakes someone tickles your palm with his/her finger, keep a good eye on "it," and don't let your pupils waver.

Sneaky Smoker

A man was sitting at a bar smoking a cigarette. Every time he exhaled, the lady sitting behind him would politely cough. After an hour he had enough and turned to her and said: "Lady, you sure are sensitive, I smoke two packs of cigarettes a day and don't have a cough like that."

Public scrutiny of smokers has become so overwhelming to some that they are now fighting back. They don't care about second hand smoke, they want to inhale the first hand. They believe anyone can stop smoking, but it takes a very strong will to face lung cancer. When convictions and addictions mix, you know there is going to be trouble.

They have drawn the line at airline no smoking policies. After the captain has turned off the seat belt sign, the smokers go straight to the toilets. They moisten a paper towel that they pat around until it sticks over the detector. Smokers can take four or five big puffs without causing any problems because they exhale into the sink that has a suction device. They even dispose their cigarette down the drain. The only exposure to getting caught occurs when they leave the restroom. If no one is around, they are home free. If someone is waiting at the door, they cough and say in a low serious voice: "Damn it, someone has been smoking in there."

The airplanes do not have cameras in the restrooms, so it's very difficult to prove who was smoking. Due to many unpleasant experiences

with confrontation, airline employees have learned
they are not getting combat pay. So generally the
worst they give is an ominous warning that comes
to nothing. After all, some say that second-hand
smoke is second-hand cool.

Twenty-First Century Phobias

We have all had *super glue* stick our thumb and
index finger together for a fraction of a second until
we pull them apart. Super glue was invented to
seal wounds quickly in Vietnam; it's more skin
friendly than you might think. You can wait longer
than a fraction of a second and still pull your fingers apart.

If you have cavities and I *chew tin foil*, it will creep
you out.

Let's say you're sitting at a park bench and a
maintenance worker unexpectedly starts a *power tool*
behind you, it will make you jump.

Getting Even

Some people turn the other cheek to get most of
the blanket. These people only believe in karma if
someone cheats them. A person I once knew, who
believed in karma, use to go around punching
people in the mouth asking them "what they did to
deserve that." There is probably nothing more bitter than an opportunist who miscalculates. Disappointed opportunists are notorious for "get even"
schemes.

House Down

When the victim is away on vacation, the hustler rents a truck and puts a little mud on the license plate. Wearing sunglasses and a fake mustache he pulls up to the day labor meeting with a job offer. He tells every able bodied man with a hammer to get in the back of his truck, and that he will pay each of them twenty dollars an hour for four hours work.

He takes them to the victim's house and says: "I'm going to build a new home on this land. I need each one of you to start helping me knock this house down. I will be back in four hours to pick you up and pay you. So start hammering away and I'll see you soon." Of course he never returns.

Box of Rocks

The less mean spirited revenge seekers might send a box of rocks C.O.D.

Merry Christmas

Some of them wait until two days after Christmas and place an ad in the newspaper that says: "Will buy your used Christmas tree for five dollars." They put their victim's address in the ad.

This happened to a friend of mine once. Hundreds of people brought their Christmas trees. The Boy Scouts had truckloads. He spent two weeks arguing and apologizing to people who ended up throwing their trees in his yard and driving off in anger.

Winning a Fight

Often clever people and those who use the information in this book for the wrong purposes, can't get a fake ID, or out of town fast enough, so they have to fight.

When these situations occur the hustler goes straight into the weasel: letting the shoulders hang down; acting wimpy hoping to avoid the confrontation; cocking the head and stuttering pathetically.

This makes the aggressor overconfident. If there's no way of getting out of the fight, the hustler springs the hardest punch he can muster to his opponent's nose and takes off running for his life.

Easy Jail Time

Most wise guys end up in jail. The clever ones know how to type because typing is the easiest of trustee jobs.

How to Get Everything You Want

Can you keep a secret? So can I. But if you find the answer, let's write a book together.

ABOUT THE AUTHOR

Fact is stranger than fiction. A brain trust of Hollywood's most talented creative minds could never conceive the cultural icon that is Jim Rose—an internationally renowned performance artist, controversial author and Snake Oil salesman extraordinaire.

Rose burst into national prominence during the 1992 Lollapalooza tour, garnering raves on MTV and publications ranging from the Wall Street Journal to Rolling Stone. The venerable rock 'n' roll magazine called the Jim Rose Circus "the absolute must-see act." *USA Today* termed Rose's troupe "Lollapalooza's word of mouth hit attraction." The quick witted show became the darling of high and low brow society alike.

Prior to Lollapalooza, Rose honed his spectacular and exotic skills throughout Europe and North America. His shows are revered as a mind bending thrill ride. Rose leads and misleads a rapt audience on a journey rife with black magic secrets, idiotic achievements and dangerous exploits. It explores and sometimes exposes the intricate distinctions between man, monster and dumbass. Performances are infused with Rose's wicked wit, hilarious asides and stunning feats. He delights the audience with a charismatic tongue-in-cheek style reminiscent of the glory days of P.T. Barnum.

Since the early Nineties, Rose has headlined seven world tours and released a self titled video (on Rick Rubin's American Recordings) which quickly became a cult classic. A perennial favorite among the most influential musical artists in the world, Rose was invited in 1994 to tour with Nine Inch Nails and a then unknown Marilyn Manson. Tours with Korn and Godsmack followed.

By 1998, Rose and his Circus were astonishing the masses on another world tour and on other levels. First, Rose was featured as a guest star on *The X-Files*. Then his eccletic lifestyle and compelling personality became the basis for a provocative literary work. His book, *Freak Like Me* was released by Bantam Doubleday Dell and ending up on several best-seller lists. As reported in the LA Times and Daily Variety, he has sold the book's movie rights to White Peach Productions and scheduled to start shooting at the end of this year. Later, Rose's legendary persona garned a new degree of infamy thanks to hit TV show *The Simpsons*—where Homer joined Rose's circus as the Human Cannonball in a truly memorable episode.

Rose's recent accolades include being the top ticket of the Melbourne (Australia), New Zealand and

Edinburgh (Scotland) Fringe and Comedy Festivals. Jim Rose can also be played. He is the popular Psymon on Play Station's new SSX Tricky and SledStorm 2, both EA products. His TV series "The Jim Rose Twisted Tour" can be seen in reruns all over the world.

Rose's cutting edge business acumen has been noticed organically: *Wall Street Journal* cover story, *Fast Company* magazine cover and featured in the new book *The Deviant's Advantage*. He has been hired to consult for numerous corporations including Microsoft and regularly assists public relations firms with pop culture campaigns and strategy. Rose served as a spokesperson for Gordon's Gin and his creative exploits were detailed in the book *Improperganda—the Art of the Publicity Stunt*. He has just wrapped as an actor for the movie "Doubting Riley" produced by HBO's "Project Greenlight" alumni.

Rose currently resides in Las Vegas, busily preparing his next literary project, planning a world tour, consulting and playing poker. On the side, he even finds time to extol the virtues of Snake Oil.

A Few Words about the Cover Portrait of Jim Rose

In a world of digital technology, Gail Potocki was trained in the manner of the Old Masters, learning to blend the brushwork of Rembrandt with the ideals of the 19th century Symbolists. Seeing Jim's circus performance and recognizing his passion for the lost arts is what led Gail to appreciate Jim as a fellow anachronism and inspired her to create his portrait. Much like the lemurs assisting his pose, Gail views Jim as an exotic and nearly extinct creature.

Gail, who was the First Prize winner of the 2002 International Symbolist Art show "The Dreamer and the Dreamed" and in 2003 won the top prize of Choix des Juges at Brave Destiny, the world's largest exhibition of Surrealist Art, continues to work in Chicago, finding inspiration in building her collection of 19th century mystical Art Nouveau artifacts.